WATERCOLOURS

'Painting and Drawing' Series

Distributors in U. K.

FOUNTAIN PRESS LTD.
65, Victoria Street, Windsor, Berkshire SL4 1EH
Telephone: Windsor 56959

WATERCOLOURS

JOSE M. PARRAMON / G. FRESQUET

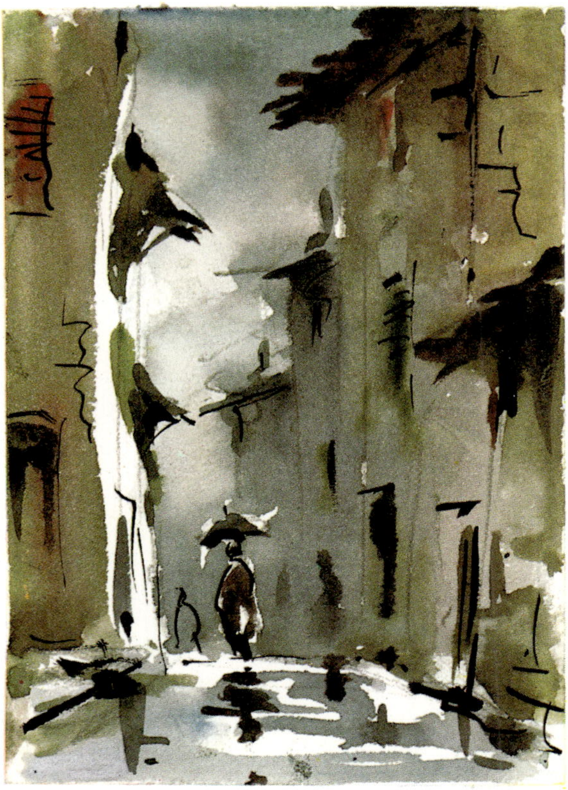

Parramón editions

Published by Parramón Ediciones, S.A.
Lepanto, 264 -4.° - Barcelona - (Spain)

Second impression

Register Book Number: 785
Legal Deposit: B-15.390-84
ISBN: 0 86343 040 6

Printed in Spain by
GENERAL GRAFIC, S.A.
Caspe, 172 - Barcelona-13 - Spain

Distributed in the United Kingdom by
FOUNTAIN PRESS LTD.
65, Victoria Street,
Windsor, Berkshire SL41 EH

CONTENTS

When and How ... 9

GENERAL FEATURES OF MONOCHROME ... 12

Method and skill ... 14
Brief description of materials ... 15
How to mount and stretch paper ... 17
How to paint a regular, uniform grey ... 18
How to remove colour from a recently painted area ... 20
Painting a grey area ... 22
Wash painting ... 23
How to paint a shaded area ... 24
Marking out white areas in advance ... 25
Superimposing tones or coats ... 26
The essential features of good monochrome ... 27

PRATICAL EXERCISES IN MONOCHROME ... 28

PAINTING WITH WATERCOLOUR (I) ... 35

Description of materials ... 35
The potential of watercolour ... 44
Theory, technique and skill of watercolour painting ... 46
Using just the three primary colours ... 49
The «wet watercolour» style ... 51
Over-painting and marking out white areas ... 53

PRACTICE IN PAINTING IN WATERCOLOUR ... 57

Only three colours... and black ... 57
The first exercise ... 59
A specific exercise using three colours only ... 66
Fresquet paints a still-life ... 70

PAINTING WITH WATERCOLOUR (II)

Painting with watercolour, using every colour ... 77
Choice and preliminary study of the subject ... 77
General rules for composing a landscape ... 79
  Fresquet paints a «dry» watercolour ... 84
  Fresquet paints a «wet» watercolour ... 94

The final test: ... 103
  First step: composition ... 105
  First stage: painting the sky and general tones ... 106
  Second stage ... 117
  Third and last stage ... 117

And that was painting in watercolour ... 118

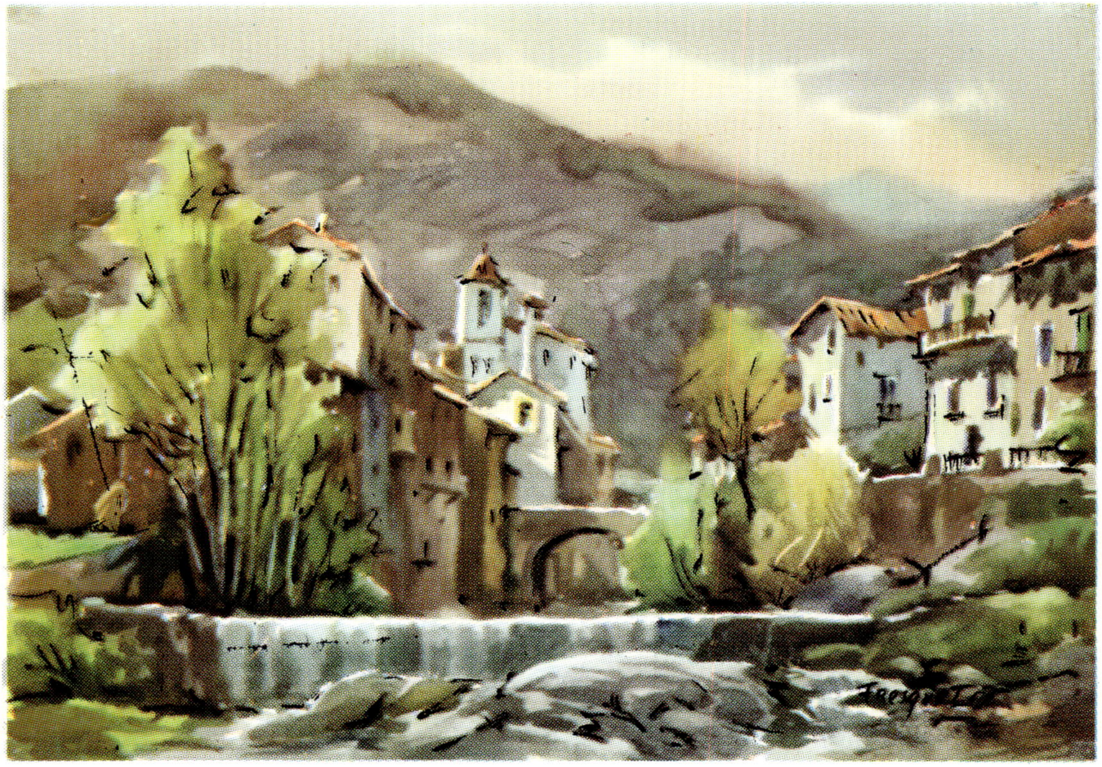

PAINTING IN WATERCOLOUR

The Parramón Instituto is pleased to acknowledge the assistance of the artist Guillermo Fresquet, who was joint author of the text and painted most of the illustrations in this book.

ADVISER: GUILLERMO FRESQUET BARDINA

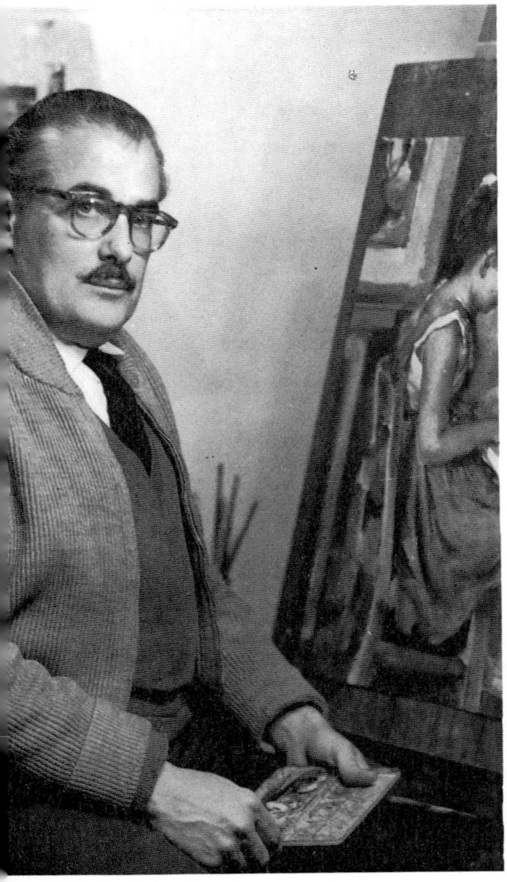

Guillermo Fresquet began his art studies at the Barcelona Art School as a pupil of the famous artist Luis Muntaner, who was then a professor at that School. Like most art students Fresquet first practised oil-painting, but very soon realised that watercolour was a more rapid medium for reproducing the spontaneity of the transient moment or, in his own words, could capture «the fleeting glow of the dawn, of the sunset, the haze over fields, producing a sense of depth, the movements of a horse or person, etc., all of which can be caught only in a rapid sketch, using material which is easy to mix and quick to dry, namely watercolour, with its ability to reproduce the freshness of experience...» Fresquet studied and practised eagerly and soon won a position as one of the most gifted artists in this field. He held his first exhibition as early as 1946 in the Sala Velasco, Barcelona, and then during the following years exhibited in the Sala Rovira. To the acclaim of the critics and public he has exhibited his work in Madrid, Barcelona, Valencia and other Spanish provinces, as well as in France, where his pictures have been included in National Salons and Exhibitions. Fresquet's mastery of watercolour has won him numerous prizes and medals, including in particular: 1950, Prize in the Llavaneras landscape exhibition; 1954, first medal from the Cataluña Watercolourists' Society; 1954, Special prize at the 1st Montblanche Biennial; 1955, first prize at the Deputation of Tarragona Province; 1956, Society's Medal at the Second Montblanche Biennial; 1962, First medal from the Cataluna Watercolourists' Society; 1963, first prize from the Barcelona Municipal Government, etc.

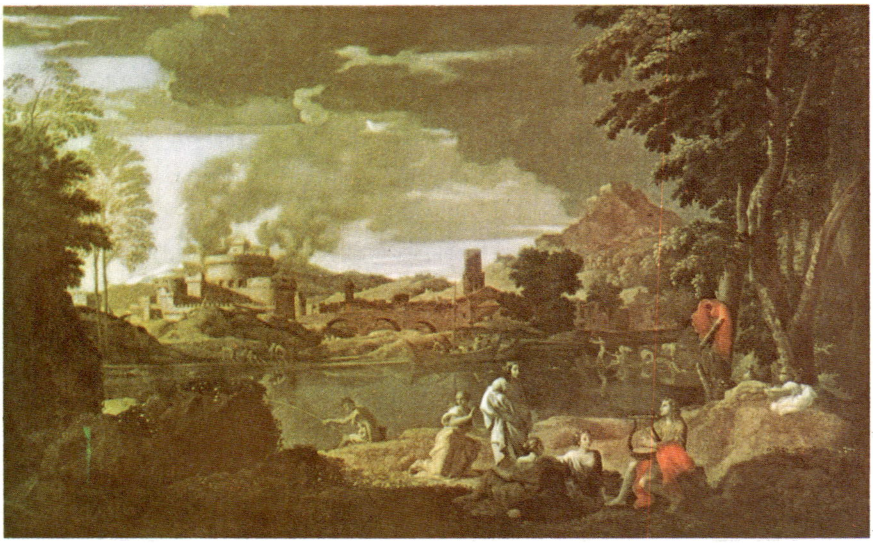

1

Within the context of the Neoclassical movement in the 18th Century, two excellent interpreters of landscapes with classical ruins were Poussin and Lorrain (above and left).

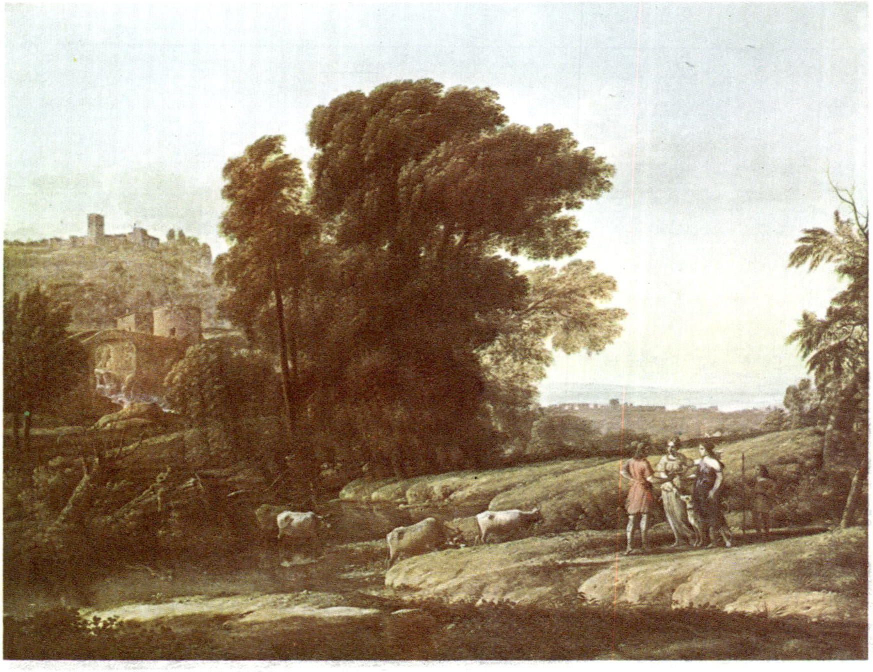

2

WHEN AND HOW

Around the middle of the eighteenth century the English discovered Rome.

At that period George II of the Hanoverian dynasty was determined to transform England, which had always been an agricultural country, into an industrial and commercial nation: factories replaced the family workshop and trade sought new scope abroad and in the colonies. Hundreds of merchants, industrialists, intellectuals and aristocrats travelled to and fro across the Channel between England and the old Continent.

Short history of watercolour painting.

It became fashionable to travel.

The obligatory route passed through France, Switzerland and Italy with Rome as its final destination. In fashionable London society it was vital to be able to say how things were in Rome and that one had seen the Coliseum, the Arch of Titus or the Baths of Caracalla, which were «very well, thank you».

... it was during the 18th Century in the period of the neoclassical artistic movement.

This was the century of the Grand Tour and also the century of the «Classical Tradition». Indeed, the whole of Europe, the entire world, looked towards Rome and Athens. Every sphere of art — painting, sculpture and architecture — took inspiration from Classicism and Antiquity, imitating the external forms of Grecian and Greco-Roman art. It was the period of *the artistic movement known as «Neoclassicism»*.

Poussin and Lorrain, the first landscape painters.

The «Discovery» of Rome by the English had a considerable influence upon the taste of the upper classes. When passing through Paris on their way to Italy the English could see, for instance, the astonishing landscapes of Nicolas and Gaspar Poussin and Claude, Lorrain, celebrated artists who are considered to be the first to paint nature as it is, taking their easels out of their studios into the open air. The English, being so fond of nature, were fascinated by the novelty and originality of the subjects painted by Poussin and Lorrain who, in keeping with the neoclassical style of that period, composed landscapes of which a major theme was nearly always Ancient Roman ruins or monuments: both artists moved to Rome when 28 and 27 respectively and lived there for the rest of their lives, proving how great was Rome's attraction during that period.

Partiality for landscapes with classical ruins.

The influence of antiquity's forms upon painting, sculpture and architecture in France, Switzerland and Italy, the originality of landscapes painted «al fresco», the landscapes' theme of classical ruins, the English partiality for nature... all this seemed to coagulate so that, on reaching Rome, the English tourist wanted to take away a pictorial souvenir, a painting or sketch, of the Eternal City.

At first these paintings were commissioned from Italian artists, but when these became unable to satisfy the demand, the English had the idea of producing large prints of the Coliseum, Trajan's Column or Hadrian's Mausoleum. The prints were made in a single colour, black, from magnificent copper engravings.

These famous English prints became fashionable throughout the United Kingdom.

Soon the reproductions were painted by hand with coloured transparent washes. The hand-colouring became increasingly important until the prints seemed to be painted rather than drawn. However, only a limited number of colours could be used: the prints were hand-painted and standardized, using a maximum of five colours. Eventually a young English artist called Joseph Mallord William Turner painted a picture using the full range of transparent colours without basing it upon a black print, that is to say directly upon a pencil sketch.

The first water-colours: colouring copper engravings.

So watercolour painting was born.

To be fair, we should mention that the method of colouring a sketch with transparent colours had already been tried by the Renaissance and Baroque artists. A famous example of this is Rembrandt's sketches done with a pen and two colours, one — usually sepia — being diluted with water and applied with a brush to emphasize the contours of objects. Water-colours are probably a derivation from this type of sketch, which in technical language are called «monochrome aquarelles». But, strictly speaking, the real historical and artistic innovators and promoters of watercolour painting were the English artists and particularly Joseph Mallord William Turner.

The monochrome aquarelles of the Renaissance and Baroque periods — forerunners of present-day watercolour painting.

3

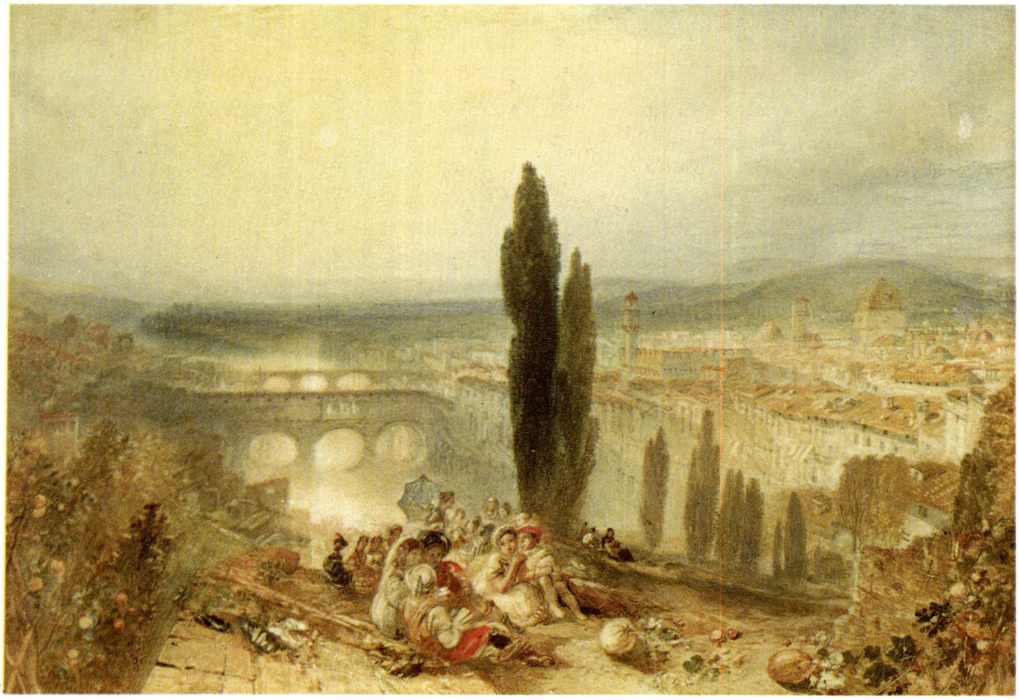

J. M. William Turner. *Watercolour*. London, British Museum.

The new process could not have found a better supporter than William Turner. Famous at the age of twenty-four, unanimously elected to the Royal Society of Arts and an outstanding landscape artist who is recognised as the most immediate precursor of French Impressionism, Turner was one of England's greatest painters: he painted an enormous number of works both in oils and in watercolour and was an innovator and outstanding master of the latter method, imitated and admired by all the artists of his period: Paul Sandby, John Cozens, Constable, de Wint, Colman, and so on. By their superb examples, Turner and his contemporaries made watercolour «the most popular method of painting in England».

William Turner

Later, at the end of the 19th Century, watercolour painting lost its popularity, perhaps because it tried to emulate and surpass oils. Finally, in the second decade of this century, watercolouring underwent a revival and gained a leading position as a special technique.

4

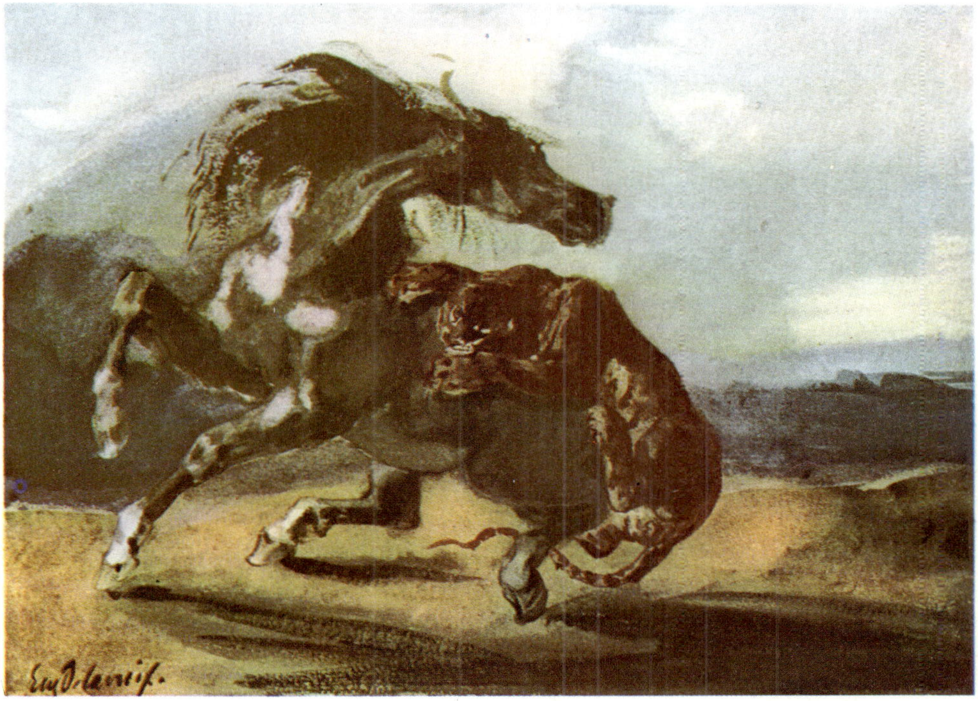

Eugène Delacroix. — *Horse attacked by a panther.* Paris, Musée du Louvre.

GENERAL FEATURES OF MONOCHROME

It is sometimes said that monochrome is *drawing* because from only one colour it produces a whole range of dark, medium and light *tones*. It is also maintained that monochrome is *painting* since it is argued that, although it is only one hue, it employs colour and is done with a brush, which as an instrument implies painting rather than drawing. Some people call monochrome a «single-tint» drawing and others compare it with tempera painting.

One fact is certain: monochrome is an introduction to watercolouring. As we have said earlier, mastery of watercolouring is impossible without knowledge and practical experience of monochrome. Therefore we logically feel that it is not only advisable, but essential, to begin these instructions with practical study of monochrome.

Definition of the medium.

So let us begin by defining this method:

Monochrome is an artistic process characterised primarily by drawing and painting with only one colour diluted to various degrees with water: this produces the tones of the model with the help of the white paper, that is by transparency or colour washes.

In painting, the term «washes» means applying a coat of transparent colour, either directly onto the surface, in this case the paper, or onto another colour, producing a specific colour or tone or strengthening the existing hue.

Definition of «washes».

Wash-painting can be done equally well with one watercolour or Indian ink diluted with water. When diluted, both types are transparent. Black is generally used for monochrome but, particulary in the artistic world, it is possible to use other dark colours such as dark blue, a dark bottle green, sienna, etc. However, monochrome in the purest sense of the term does not allow retouching or re-painting with white paint. In other words:

Black is generally used.

In monochrome, whites have to be obtained from the paper by means of areas left blank for that purpose.

Whites must be obtained by using blank areas.

This implies, in fact, that water is employed solely to dilute and weaken the tone of the colour in order to obtain greys and muted colours. When using watercolours either rain-water or tap-water is satisfactory. With Indian ink the water must be distilled or boiled. Watercolours are softer than Indian ink, so that it is much easier to obtain muted colours and weaker tones with water, as we shall see when we come to the section on method and materials.

With watercolour: running water.

With Indian ink: distilled water.

The same brushes are generally used for monochrome as for watercolouring: they are made of sable, ichneumon or fur from a cow's ear. A set of three brushes, Nos. 2, 6 and 10, are sufficient for monochrome.

Brushes

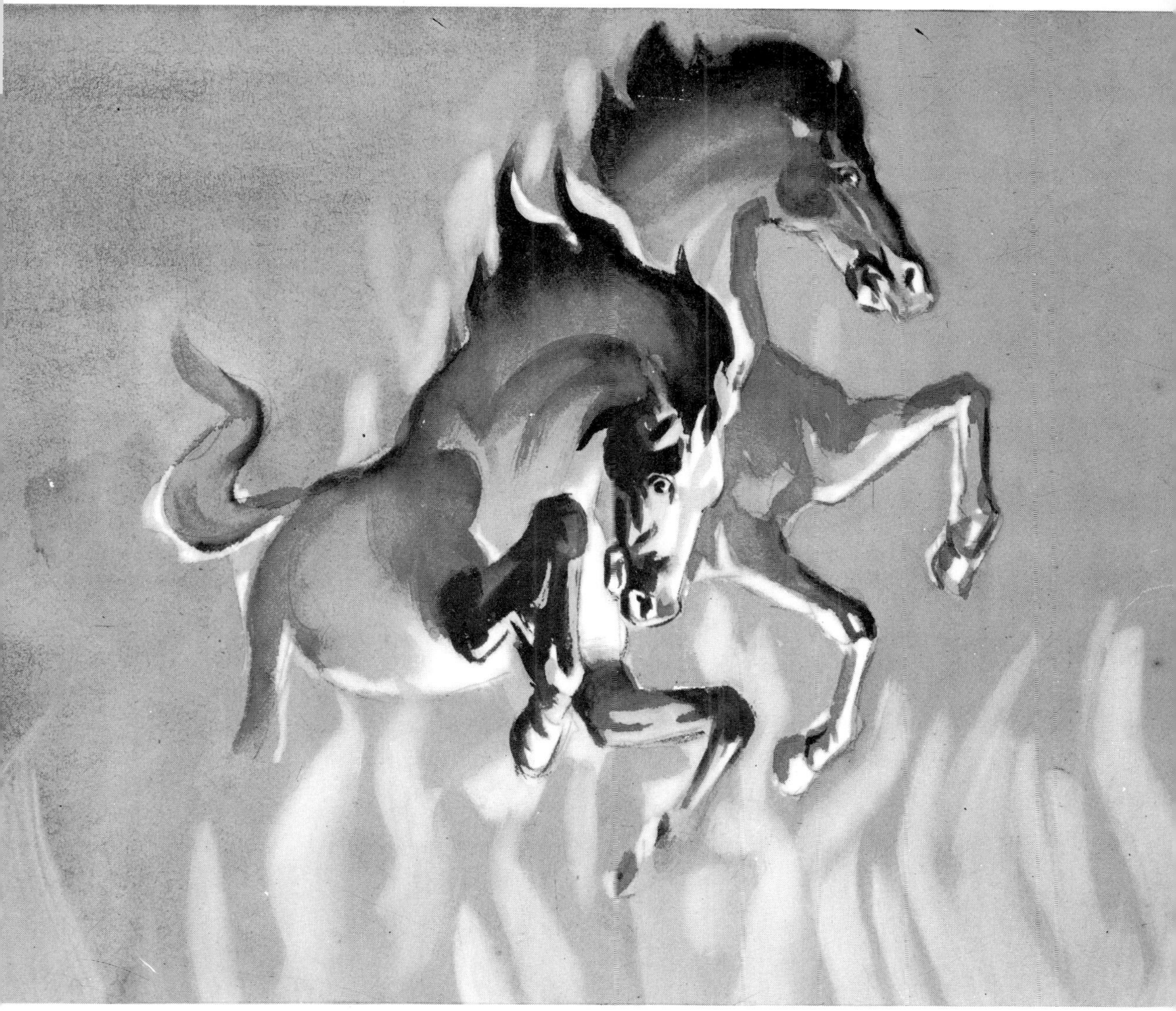

Monochrome has a practically unlimited number of uses. It is widely employed in commercial art, both for advertisements and for producing illustrations or sketches for brochures, cards, catalogues, etc.

In the purely artistic field, it is a widely used medium for preliminary studies — especially for figures and landscapes — designs for murals and decoration in general.

Finally, we can say that it forms an essential introduction to mastering the difficult art of water-colour — the subject of this book.

For professional painters it is also essential to have one or more watercolour palettes, a kind of china saucer for dissolving the colour. However, for our purposes in this book, an ordinary dessert plate or even a piece of paper may serve as a palette: we shall deal with this in the section on method and skill.

Watercolour palettes.

We also need a glass jar or bottle for the water and a clean rag for cleaning, and drying the brushes which, as we shall see, must be done frequently. It is also advisable to have clean blotting-paper to remove any excess watercolour when necessary.

Water-jar.

Monochrome is done on good-class drawing-paper, such as Canson or Whatman, which must be thick enough not to lose its shape when moistened. Its grain and priming must be such that regular greys and shaded areas can be obtained. Very smooth or very thickly primed papers with a shiny or satinlike surface cannot be used for monochrome. To prevent any disappointments, I would recommend you always to buy the same brand or class of paper once you have found it satisfactory. If you are in doubt, before sketching out the subjet, test the paper by painting some greys and shaded areas on a piece: this will enable you to check the paper's absorption of water and the firmness and consistency of the fibre, etc.

Paper

We can sum up the potential of monochrome in the artistic field by saying that it is particularly suitable for landscape and figure studies or pictures, and especially figures and portraits from which it is possible to obtain pictures of a high artistic standard, whether painted with black, dark blue or sepia. Monochrome is also widely used in advertising and the graphic arts — always in black — and mastery of this technique is essential for making many illustrations for the press, brochures, cards, as well as illustrations intended for periodicals or books.

Potential of this technique

METHOD AND SKILL

As in watercolours, one of the principal elements of monochrome is water. As we know, monochrome is done with only one colour which, when it comes out of the tube (for instance a tube of black watercolour), is opaque. We have to dilute the black with water in order to «develop» it and obtain the range of greys found between the black and the whiteness of the paper. The more water, the less colour: the more water, the greater the transparency: the more water, the greater the impact of the white paper, the more we notice the whiteness of the paper and, therefore, the lighter the *tone* of the colour applied.

Primary element: water.

From this we can conclude that in order to paint a regular, uniform grey area, a little watercolour must be diluted with a certain amount of water until all the watercolour paste is dissolved and a kind of watered-down colour is obtained.

We shall do this. It has been rightly said that anyone who is able to paint a uniform grey with watercolour, water and brush, can claim that he knows how to paint in monochrome. Is it so difficult? Let's see:

First of all, let's look at each of the items used in monochrome:

Materials and utensils

One or two jars for the water
A watercolour palette or small china plate
A piece of paper for the palette
One or two brushes (Nos. 6 and 10)
A clean rag
Blotting-paper
Drawing-board
Canson paper

BRIEF DESCRIPTION OF THE MATERIALS

The water-jar

Get a much larger bottle or jar for the water. Use a glass jam-jar with a wide neck (this is important) capable of holding about a pint or more if possible. Professional artists generally use two such jars for washing their brush twice so that the brushes are cleaner and the water does not have to be changed so often. As a minor detail, remember that when filling the jar, the waterlevel should be about 3/4" below the lip so that the «load» (the amount of water taken up by the brush) can be more easily checked. Bear in mind that sometimes when touching up or darkening small areas, only a very small amount of water will be required (Fig. 6).

It is possible to use a small porcelain or china plate for dissolving the colour and preparing washes of the same tone. I must mention in this connection that personally I am not keen on using what are called «palettes», a kind of porcelain saucer with one or more hollows. I con-

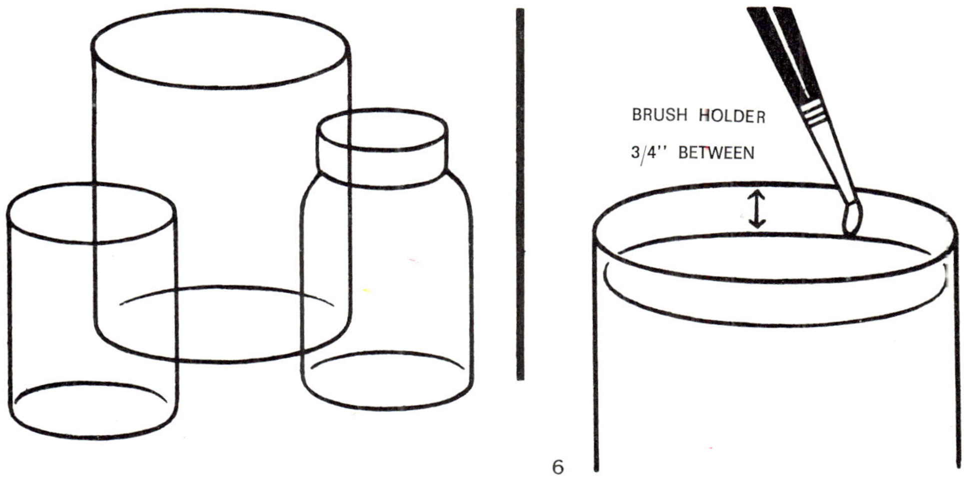

6

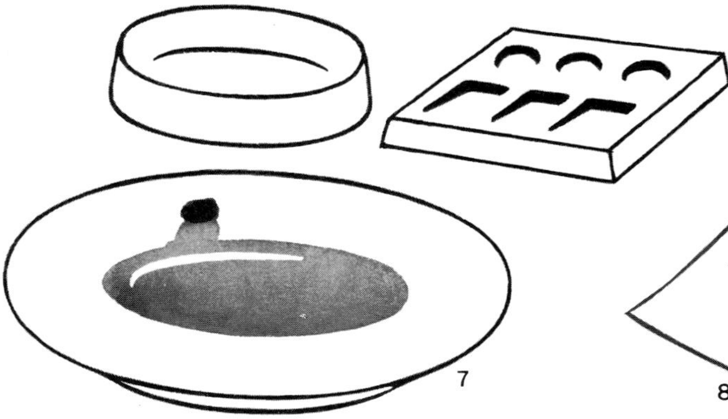

7

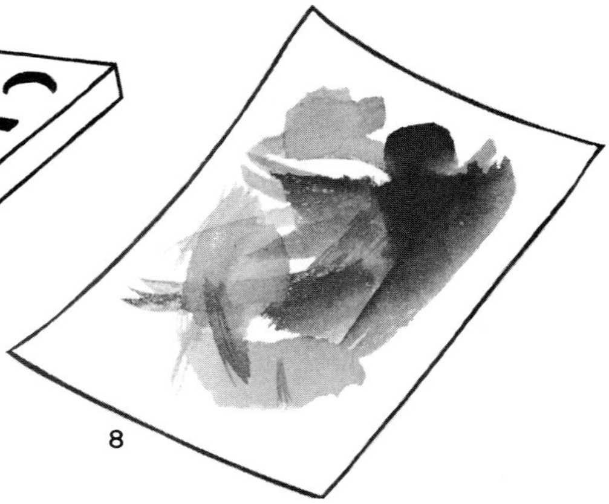

8

sider them inadequate, small and too obviously «artistic». I prefer a large plate on which I can squeeze the colour from the tube, leaving it on the edge and taking what I need for mixing with the water in the middle of the plate. It is a matter of choice. Moreover, when painting, many professionals, myself included, have acquired the habit of using a piece of paper — the same type as that used for painting the picture or illustration — squeezing a little colour on one corner and diluting it on the paper as if on a palette, testing the tone before applying it to the final picture (Figs. 7 and 8).

A china plate as a palette

Separate piece of paper as a palette.

It is not usual to paint a wash with several brushes. Generally only one brush with a high number, such as No. 10, is used, final touches being added with a finer brush for outlining and touching the smaller shapes.

Brushes

As we shall see later, the drying or absorption of the water-colour plays a constant part, either to balance and harmonize tones or to produce other effects. When adding or taking off water or watercolour in this way, the brush must always be dry and clean. A large clean piece of rag and a clean piece blotting-paper must be available.

Monochrome can be done on a tilted table or board. Bearing in mind the special characteristics of watercolouring and remembering once again that the technique is the same as that for monochrome, it is perhaps better to use a board where the angle can be varied as required. But whether you use a table or board, the important thing is that the support must be tilted.

A piece of clean rag

We have already dealt with the class and quality of the paper, so we need only mention one other important point: when moistened, paper is usually inclined to lose its shape and to cockle. This loss of smoothness is not vitally important in the professional field when the painting is going to be framed or kept in a portfolio. We must also remember that when we paint on thick paper, this defect is hardly visible. However, it becomes more important when, for instance, an illustration has to be

Support

How to avoid wrinkles and creases on the paper caused by the water.

kept and shown to a client, in which case the *presentation,* the fact of presenting an impeccable job (and in this respect the cleanness and general condition of the paper is vital), can make the client favourably or unfavourably disposed towards the work submitted. For such cases — as well as others — it is worth knowing the following method for mounting and stretching the paper.

HOW TO MOUNT AND STRETCH PAPER TO AVOID LOSS OF SHAPE CAUSED BY WATER

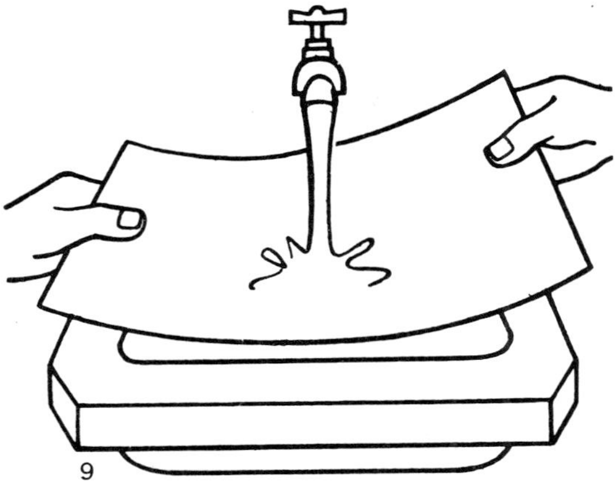

9

Materials: Besides the sheet of drawing-paper, we need a wooden board (which can be the drawing-board) and some strips of gummed tape (about 1 ½ inches wide).

Fig. 9. Begin by thoroughly wetting the drawing-paper, dipping it in a tub of water or holding it under the tap. It must be made thoroughly but not excessively wet, i.e. not done hurriedly but without leaving the paper in the water for more than three or four minutes. Too much water can damage the priming and thus the fibre and consistency of the paper.

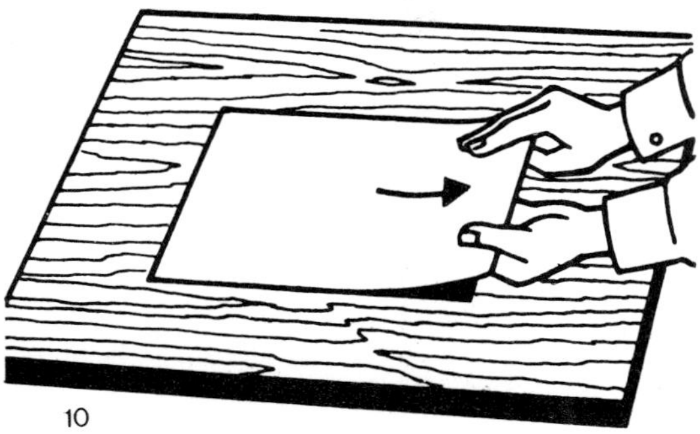

10

Fig.10. Shake off the surplus water and lay the paper on the wooden board. It is important to ensure at this point that the paper is completely flat without wrinkles along the edge. It may help to stretch it a little, pulling it at both sides as in the figure.

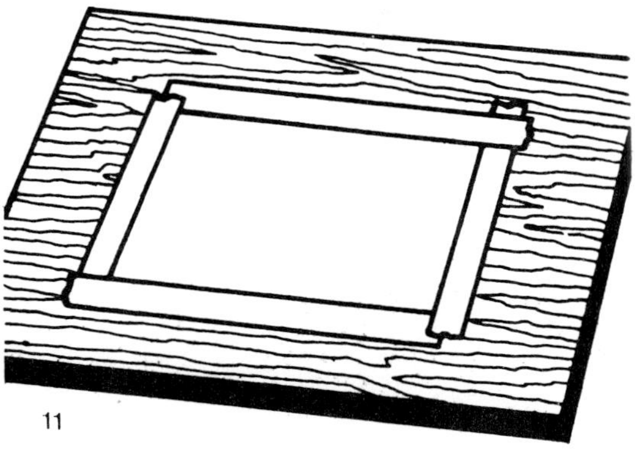

11

Fig.11. The final step is to stick the paper to the board using the strips of gummed tape, framing the paper as in the figure. Make sure that the gummed tape is of good quality, such as that normally used for packing and sealing parcels.

It is now simply a matter of waiting until the drawing paper dries completely and naturally. It is unwise to speed up this drying process by placing the paper in the sun or near a stove: it is best to dry it by placing the board in a horizontal position, laying it on a table for instance, in order to obtain uniform dryness all over the paper.

Wait until the mounted paper dries naturally

Finally, when the paper is completely dry (which takes five or six hours), it looks as taut as the skin over a drumhead and it can be painted or moistened as much as you want without producing any subsequent wrinkles. The paper is, of course, kept mounted when you are painting and, once the picture is finished, it is taken off the board with a razorblade, cutting around the edges. Talking of edges, these must be allowed for and calculated before beginning the picture, bearing in mind the wastage caused by attaching the gummed tape.

The theory upon which this simple operation for mounting and stretching the paper is based can easily be understood. When the paper is made wet, it expands or swells up: then, held by the strips of tape, it contracts when drying, remaining tight and conditioned against any subsequent loss of shape.

Theory of the method

I repeat, however, that this procedure is usually unnecessary and is only advisable, but not essential, in cases such as those described above.

After this short description of materials and their use, we shall now deal with the medium in practice, trying to paint a regular, uniform area of grey.

HOW TO PAINT A REGULAR, UNIFORM GREY

Put some black water-colour on the edge of the plate or saucer (See Fig. 7). Take a No. 10 brush... make it wet... remove it from the water almost dripping wet. Put the water from the brush on the plate: repeat this several times. Now take a little colour on your brush: dip it in the water on the plate: mix it, moving the brush in circles until all the watercolour is diluted with the water. Do this slowly and carefully, making sure that every particle is dissolved.

Preparing a quantity of wash, for painting grey

Fasten the drawing-paper to the board with drawing-pins. Trace in pencil a rectangle about 3½" x 4" on the drawing-paper and...

But wait... before painting on this grey we must check the intensity of the tone to be obtained from the watered colour on the plate.

Testing the tone

Let's see! Load the brush, wipe it on the edge of the plate and paint a patch on a separate piece of paper, testing the intensity of this grey. This is where the «palette» mentioned earlier comes in, the piece of paper which serves as a palette.

Ready? Careful now...

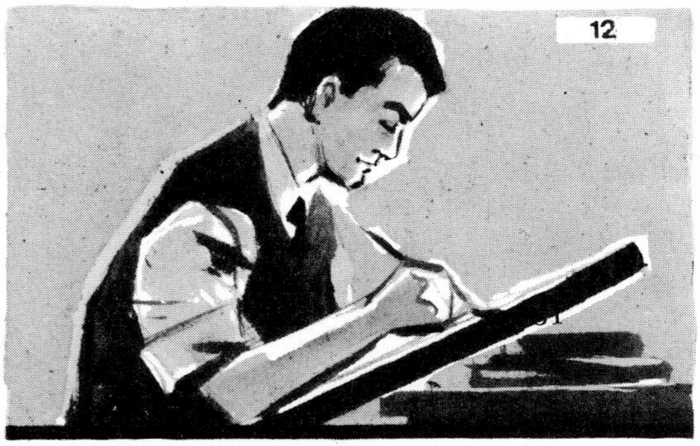

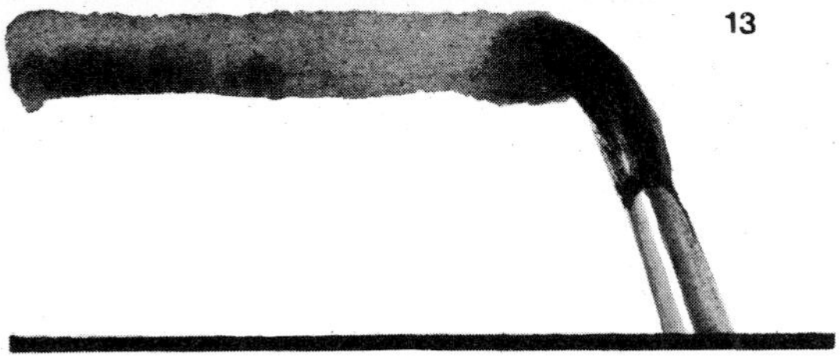

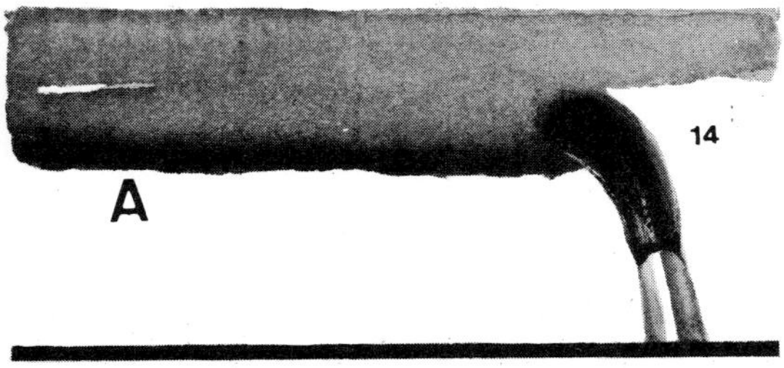

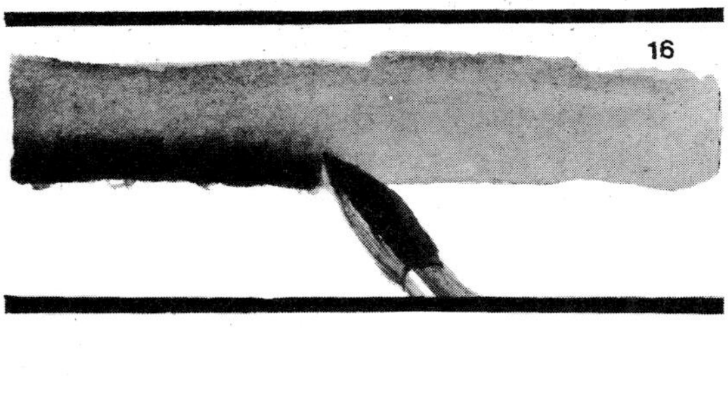

Fig. 12. Paint with the board tilted about 30°. (Well... more or less... a degree or two won't matter. You can see for yourself the right angle from this illustration).

Fig. 13. Load the brush again with the water on the plate but this time don't wipe it, bring it to the paper fully loaded (but not enough to make it drip, of course) and... *paint a horizontal stripe about 3/8" wide.*

Paint boldly in one stroke from left to right, just as if you were drawing a pencil line. And don't bother about the water accumulating along the lower edge of the strip. That's fine.

Fig. 14. Now quickly! paint another strip underneath, keeping the watercolour which accumulates along the lower edge (A).

Keep calm and everything will be all right. Paint another strip underneath the earlier ones, and another... another...

> *always keeping the beads of watercolour which enable you to keep painting over a damp surface so that the colour does not run and the coat is perfect and uniform.*

And so on to the end of the paper. But...

Fig. 15. When you reach the lower edge of the rectangle you will have surplus water-colour which must be removed. Nothing is easier.

Fig. 16. Clean the brush in clean water, keep it in the jar of water until you consider all the colour has been removed. Then dry it on the rag, wiping off the water and pressing it between your fingers with the rag as if you were combing it.

Next, place the tip of the brush on the watercolour left at the bottom edge of the grey and there you are! The brush acts as a sponge, absorbing all or part of the beads of colour (you may need to repeat this to absorb more of the liquid). Doing this properly will depend upon how much of the liquid you soak up and whether the brush is well wiped: the aim is to make the tone of this area the same as the rest.

Two final warnings: firstly, as you will have realised, the success of this process depends primarily upon: (a) the tilt of the board and (b) the amount of liquid in the brush. The lower the angle of the board, the less beads of watercolour will accumulate and this is essential if the painted area is to be covered naturally without edges: on the other hand, if the angle is too great, the beads will run. The same applies to a too large or too small brush-load. Secondly, and less important: when the tone of the grey is very strong or dark, it is not advisable to wash the brush when using it as a sponge. It is better to dry it or wipe it on the rag as I have explained but *without washing it,* in order to avoid the danger of changing and lightening the tone.

Success depends upon the angle of the board and the brush-load.

Now an important factor which can be deduced from the exercise above and which I think must be emphasized:

In monochrome as in watercolours, one usually paints from top to bottom.

Also, remember that:

In monochrome and watercolours, the brush-strokes are generally vertical.

Bear this in mind. When painting the grey area above we said that the strokes should be horizontal, moving the brush from left to right. In this case we used the most effective, rapid and safe method for painting large grey areas, but this could obviously have been done by a series of diagonal or vertical strokes, as shown in Fig. 17. It is also obvious that the *vertical* movement is most commonly used by professional painters for painting small and medium-sized areas, for blending and merging, etc. The reason for this is clear: vertical brush-strokes — following the angle of the board — are the most sensible way of obtaining and retaining the accumulation of watercolour which provides better harmonization of values and tones.

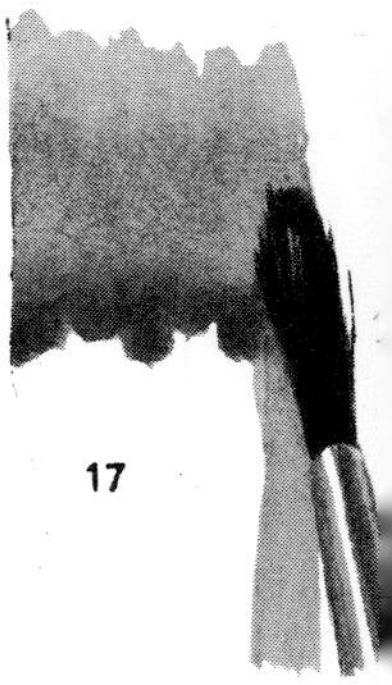

17

HOW TO REMOVE COLOUR FROM A RECENTLY PAINTED AREA OR THE ART OF USING A BRUSH AS A SPONGE

Now that we are on the subject of the beads of watercolour formed during the final stage of the grey surface and the method for removing the surplus colour, I should like to mention one of the most common tricks of the trade used in monochrome. This is the system employed by the professional artist for changing, evening out, weakening or lowering a tone, in fact for correcting it immediately after painting it: as it were, how to «take back one's words» after painting, to go over it, change it, strengthen it or lighten it, operations which are so common in modelling for bringing out the volume of objects.

Sometimes the tone is too dark or too ligtht

First of all, you must remember that even allowing for the «tone test» on the separate piece of paper used as a palette, it often happens that when the tone is transferred to the actual drawing or painting, it is too light or too dark, due perhaps to the law of simultaneous contrasts by which the tone becomes lighter or darker when put next to another shade.

Is that clear? Let's put this into practice. Imagine that... but let's see it for ourselves:

Method used

Mix together some watercolour and water — very little water this time — on the plate to make a very dark grey. Load the brush with some of this wash and paint an area of 1/2″ square. If you leave this do dry, the water will evaporate, but the amount of colour in the water will remain producing a rather dark tone (Fig. 18 A).

18 A

18 B

Repeat this operation, but this time paint the same area with the same amount of watercolour on the brush. Then wash the brush in clean water, dry it, wipe it with the rag and use it as a sponge, absorbing the surplus watercolour: apply the brush, absorb, rewash in clean water, rewipe with the rag, pass it over the painted area again, and so on, until it is more or less dry. In this way you will *not only have «evaporated» the water but also removed a large amount of the colour,* automatically weakening the tone, which is now much lighter than before (Fig. 18 B).

This experiment is important. It reminds us that the expert in monochromes constantly uses this trick to weaken, form and lower a tone. So much so, in fact, that in his eagerness, the artist frequently uses a quicker method than drying and wiping with the rag, namely by using his mouth, sucking the water from the brush! (and without spitting out the water!) Yes, you did hear — or rather read — right! Now that I am on the subject, allow me to go into it in a little more detail.

It is quite common for professionals to obtain the right watercolour and to correct, weaken or lower tones by sucking the brush, reducing the load of water in it. This method is not as nasty as it may seem. Remember especially that the brush is sucked *after it has been washed in the jar of clean water.* I repeat: AFTER IT HAS BEEN WASHED IN CLEAN WATER. And what if the water is not really clean? a bit murky? What if you make a mistake and suck it without first putting it in clean water? All I can say is that I have been sucking my brush for over twenty years and have managed to survive. One thing is certain: with this method you can measure exactly the amount of water to be taken off the brush, apart from the fact that it keeps a perfect point. But let's not exaggerate: both the professional artist and I may use the two methods, sucking and pointing the brush with the mouth and wiping it on the rag. As a teacher I must advise you to use the rag but as a friend... but that's enough, I have already explained the other method.

Removing water from the brush with the mouth

The method of sucking the brush to remove the water is commonly used by the professional artist.

PAINTING A GREY AREA AFTER MOISTENING THE SURFACE

One of the most common mistakes of an amateur when applying washes of watercolour is to «break up» a grey or shaded area. This fault is so important that it merits a separate section:

«BREAKING UP» A GREY OR SHADED AREA

When the area is left half-painted, or if little liquid is used or the grey or shaded areas are not painted quickly enough, what we call a «break» occurs, that is a well-defined change in the tone, forming an edge (Fig. 19). This break is always caused by leaving the area to dry or partially dry before it is finished. A monochrome which shows several breaks which have no connection with the picture itself denotes lack of skill.

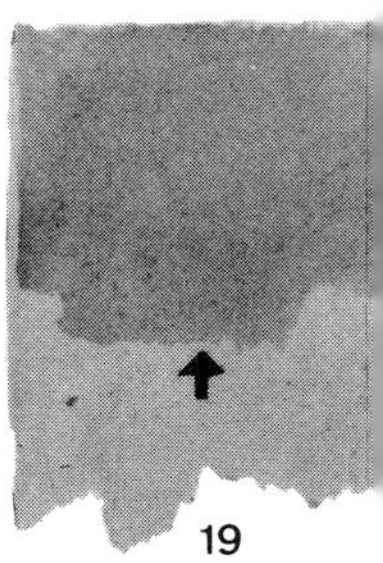

19

The break in a grey or shaded area does not usually occur — no matter how inexperienced one is — when a water-colour is used for painting the area. But it does occur when Indian ink diluted with water is used, even when the artist is an expert.

Definition and causes of «breaks»

THE BASIC DIFFERENCE BETWEEN PAINTING WITH WATERCOLOURS AND PAINTING WITH INDIAN INK DILUTED WITH WATER

As we have already said, monochromes can be painted either with watercolours or with Indian ink diluted with water. We have also emphasized that when painting with Indian ink the water must be distilled or boiled so that the colour dissolves better and the medium is fluid.

Wash-painting with Indian ink is more difficult

Until now we have been talking about and practising monochromes using black watercolour. We shall now take advantage of this section on «breaks» to examine briefly the technique of painting with Indian ink diluted with water. This is because, in practice, the only difference between painting with these two types of colour lies in the fact that Indian ink is *far firmer than watercolour or, in other words, it is not so flexible and makes the trick of removing surplus paint more difficult*, therefore forming «breaks» with remarkable ease. You must remember this in order to paint quickly and skilfully and not make a mess of things by painting with a tone darker than that needed (bear in mind that you cannot go back over it); you must apply water beforehand, keeping the areas to be painted continually moist...

On the other hand, Indian ink can produce remarkable transparency and pure tones.

An essential factor of monochromes with Indian ink

Apart from wide experience and constant practice, the technique used to compensate for the lack of fluidity of Indian ink is to moisten the area with clean water beforehand, so that the colour does not form «breaks» when applied and remains wet, which prevents it from becoming «stagnant». This method brings us to an important technique in monochromes, known as «wash painting» and for this we leave the subject of Indian ink and return to painting with black watercolour.

WASH PAINTING

«Wash painting» originally meant painting large areas like a sky in a landscape, but by analogy we apply this term to painting any large grey area which contains slight variations in tone, shaded areas with very small contrast and containing wide areas of flat tones. In such cases the artist employs this method, moistening the area involved with clean water beforehand.

This is how it is done:

Method

The area to be made grey is outlined in fine pencil. It is then moistened with clean water, using a brush or small sponge. It is very important for the water to be spread evenly, with the «loads» of clean water being measured and distributed in such a way as to produce a uniform moist coat, avoiding excessive moisture from blobs of water. The area is then painted with the prepared wash, using the method described above (the normal method for painting an even grey).

HOW TO PAINT A SHADED AREA

There are three stages in painting a shaded area with a wash:

Basic stages in painting a shaded area with a wash

1. *Paint first with the darkest tone.*
2. *Spread and dilute this tone with clean water.*
3. *Blend it with a dry brush.*

We shall see how this is done in practice, illustrating the method with the following figures:

20

Fig. 20. Imagine a wide shaded area in the form of a horizontal strip, ranging from black to white, as shown in this figure. This will be our model.

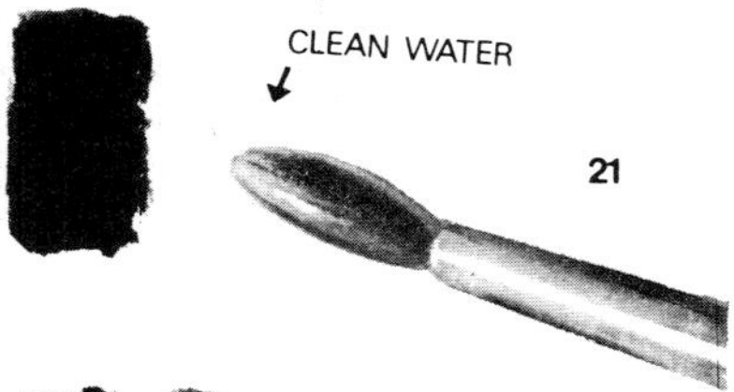

21

Fig. 21. Following the first stage («paint first with the darkest tone»), we begin by painting a black patch. As quickly as possible, we clean the brush (it would be best to have two brushes), washing it in clean water, and rapidly moistening the entire area over which the paint is to be laid...

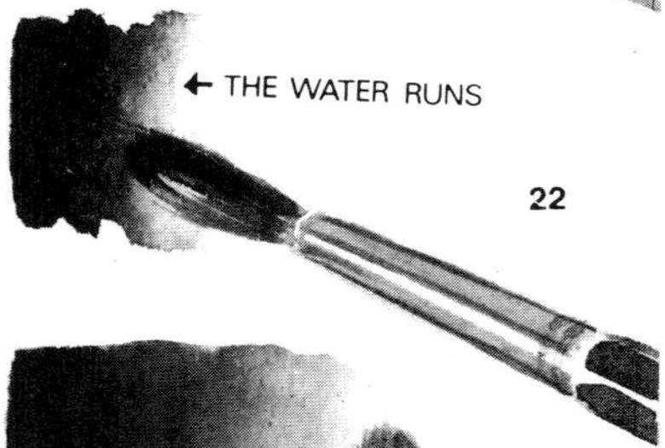

22

Fig. 22. ...until we reach the edge of the initial black patch. It is important that this patch is still wet so that we can dilute it with the water from the moistened area, spreading and weakening it with quick vertical brush-strokes. Stop before reaching half-way along the moistened area!

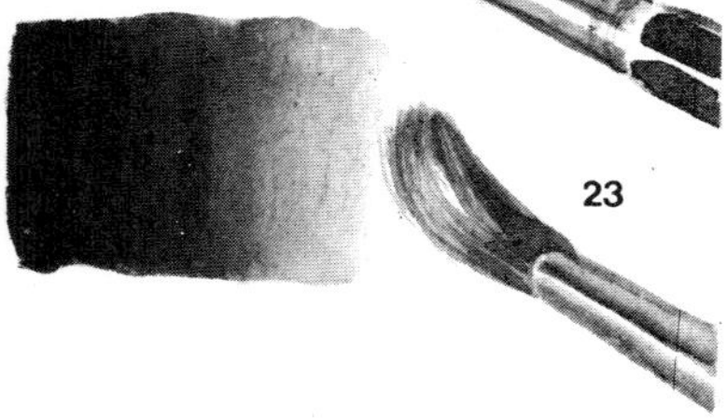

23

Fig. 23. Clean the brush again. Dry it and wipe it on the rag, take it halfway along the area, reducing the water and colour in this area.

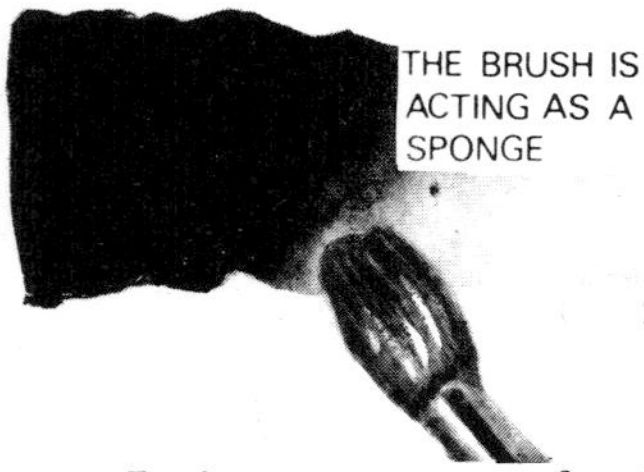

24

Fig. 24. Clean it again. Wipe it and carry on spreading the colour towards the area which is still white. Touch it up and blend the area now shaded.

It is a matter of adding and subtracting, spreading the colour and weakening it, adding water and drying it, blending, remembering that it is a continual process as long as the paper remains moist (to prevent breaks) and the dark sections are not spread to the light sections. It is always possible to add and strengthen the colour but it would be difficult to go back over it all, changing the areas painted black or grey into white. And talking of whites...

WHEN WASH-PAINTING THE WHITE AREAS MUST BE MARKED OUT IN ADVANCE

There is no white paint: we cannot paint with a white colour. White is the actual paper. It must be marked out at the start.

System for «uncovering» white in a dark area

In some cases, however, in order to obtain not white but very pale greys, it is possible to use a method similar to that described when we were explaining how to lower a tone by absorbing the water and colour in a specific area.

Imagine an area painted with a very dark grey — even black, if you wish — some time ago and now completely dry. Suppose that a small shape in a lighter tone than the background has to be shown in this area, a star for example. So, to produce a light grey there, since there is no pure white:

Fig. 25. Begin by loading the brush with absolutely clean water and make the area in question very wet by forming a thick bead of water.

Fig. 26. Leave the water there for several minutes, long enough to moisten and loosen the colour under it.

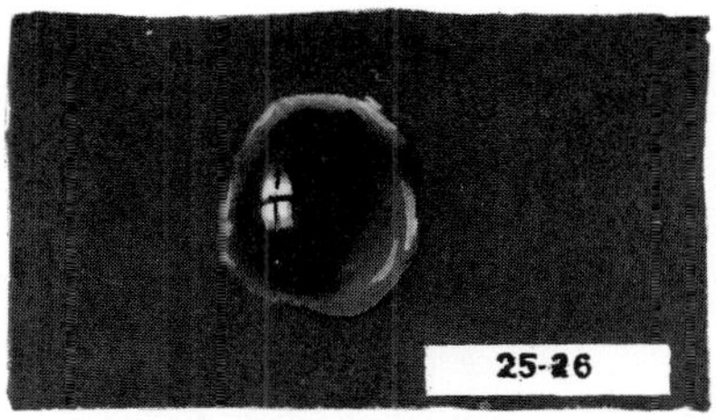

25-26

Fig. 27. Now apply the brush, trying to dilute the colour with the water formed over it. This takes some time and patience, stroking it gently with the brush so that the colour is loosened and diluted with the water.

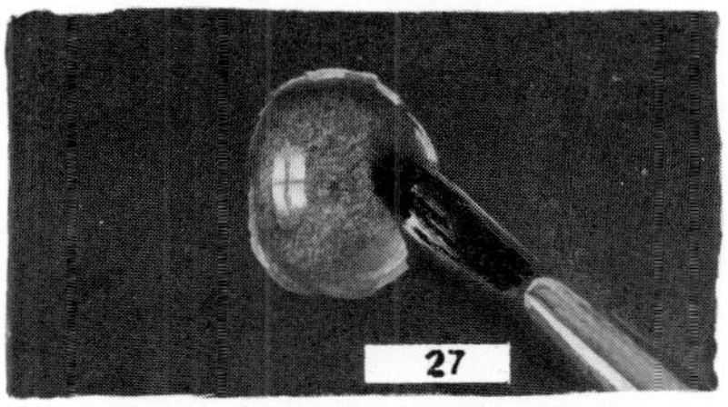

27

Fig. 28. When you think the colour has dissolved, clean the brush again, dry it and wipe it with the rag. Now begin to absorb the diluted colour, clean the brush again, absorb more colour, and so on until the area is practically dry. This will produce a lighter tone than the surrounding area.

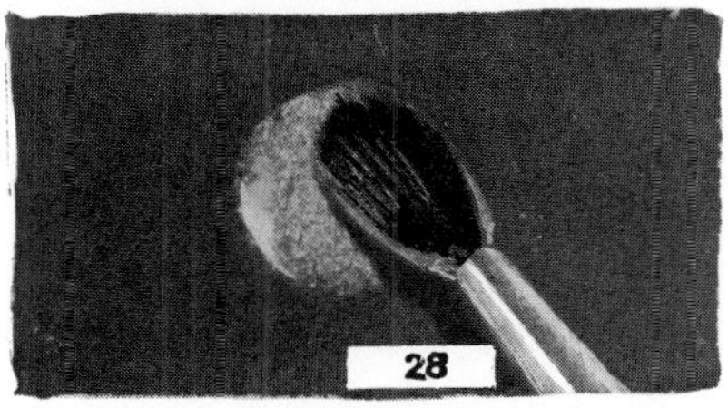

28

Fig. 29. All you need to do now is to touch up the edges (imagine in this case that you want to produce a bright star on a dark background) and the job is finished.

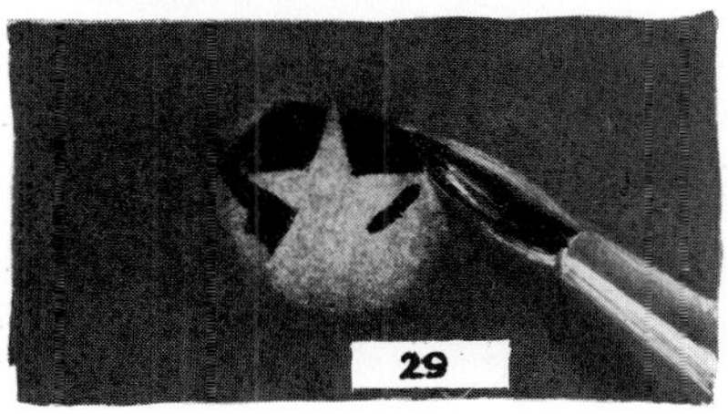

29

TO SUPERIMPOSE TONES OR COATS

When painting with washes or watercolours it is customary to superimpose tones, intensifying the colour values, adapting the painted shape and creating contrasts: we must think of the artist as painting in increasing levels, applying one coat over another. For instance, to produce the shape and volume of a cube, the correct method is:

30

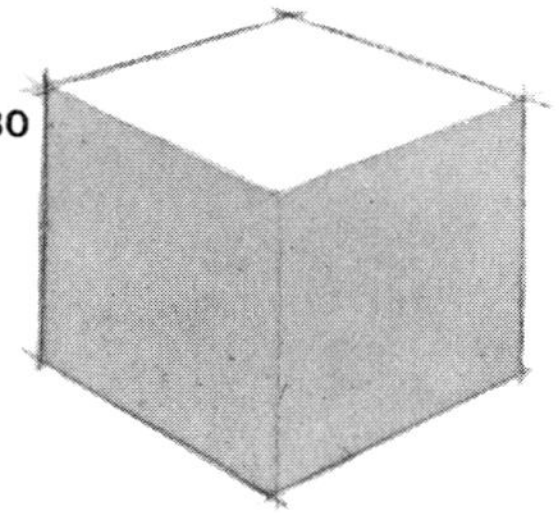

Fig. 30. First paint the entire shadowed area with a grey coat, in one tone.

31

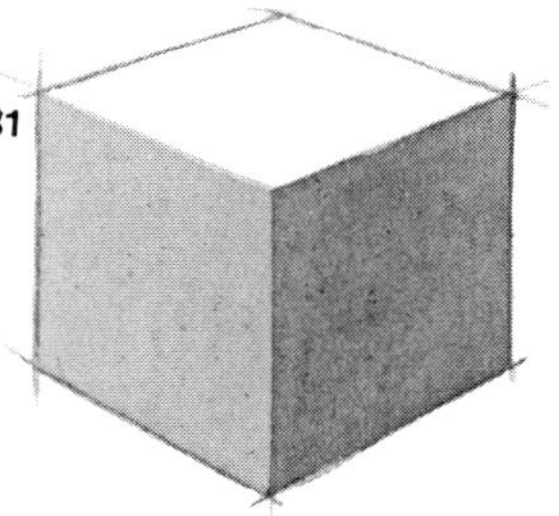

Fig. 31. Wait for it to dry and then apply a new coat or wash over the darkest plane.

32

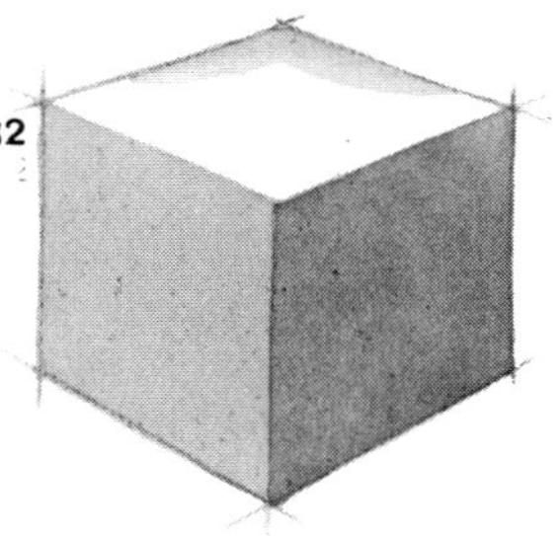

Fig. 32. Finally, to finish the picture, paint at the furthest corner of the upper surface a narrow strip of light grey...

33

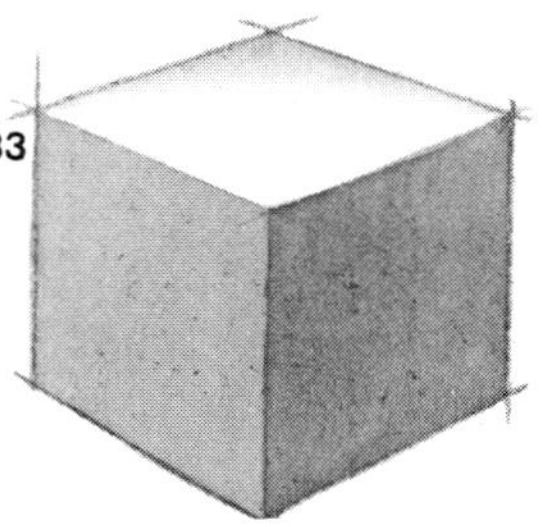

Fig. 33. ...which is quickly shaded while it is still wet, by applying the brush with clear water, diluting the original strip with water, blending it by absorbing the water, etc...

When painting one tone over another, the only thing to remember is that the first must be completely dry. The second coat must also be applied rapidly so as not to spoil or disturb the first.

THE ESSENTIAL FEATURE OF GOOD MONOCHROME

By explaining how the tones or coats are superimposed and saying that an artist paints in increasing levels, we may have given you the idea that monochrome is: obtaining a picture by superimposing many coats of colour, increasing the tone slowly, wash after wash, until the required intensity is produced. That's wrong! A good monochrome is quite the opposite. Let's get this clear:

> **The essential feature of good monochrome is to paint the required tones immediately with as few coats as possible.**

Admittedly, that is not easy. But that's where the value lies: with your ability to accept the risk and hit the mark at first — or second — shot. It is this which produces a genuinely artistic and skilful work, a fresh, spontaneous and assured monochrome, quite different from an amateur's work, unassured, hesitant, laborious and badly finished.

Need for constant practice

To acquire this skill and assurance you must paint many monochromes, practising and learning. The actual technique on which you can base such skill is contained in these paragraphs and in the practical exercises we are now going to give you. But genuine knowledge must be gained by painting dozens of monochromes, studying the technique and skill of monochrome over and over again.

PRACTICAL EXERCISES IN MONOCHROME

To improve your knowledge, we shall now give a series of practical exercises in monochrome. Use these to take your first steps in this medium.

In the shapes and models given below we have tried to include all the technical difficulties which may occur in this medium so that, when you have done them perfectly, you can claim to be capable of dealing with any subject no matter how complicated it may be. Because, in practice, what other difficulties can occur when producing monochrome landscapes, a still-life or figures? Aren't these and every other type of image a combination of shapes depicted in flat grey and shaded areas, cylinders and spheres? So treat these exercises with the respect they deserve. When practising them, keep in mind that they are essential and the final stage of your apprenticeship.

Exercise A. Monochrome of a book

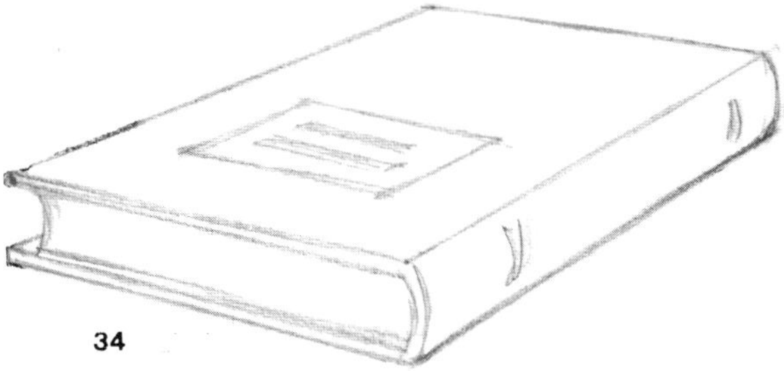

34

First of all you need a good initial outline, copying an actual book if you wish, and, if necessary, using a ruler and setsquare. Work out the line of the horizon, the lines of perspective, etc. You must produce a simple but completely accurate sketch (Fg. 34).

Now begin by painting planes A and B with a flat, grey wash, taking care not to go over the outline. Notice that you must keep the small area of light at the point marked (a'). Also paint the smooth shading at the upper edge of the spine (b'), simply by cleaning the brush, moistening the shaded area while the grey wash is still wet, then soaking it up and blending it with some more brush-strokes, etc. (Fig. 35).

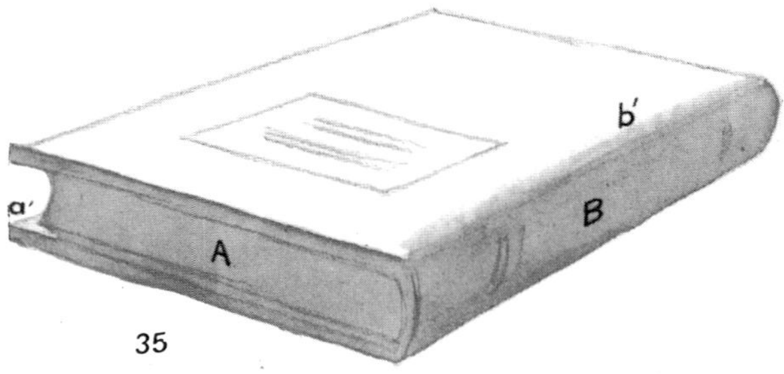

35

The next stage is to paint the plane C, the cover (Fig. 36), leaving out the square for the title.

Good, when the entire plane is moistened, place a stroke of grey wash at the furthest corner, more or less as mark-

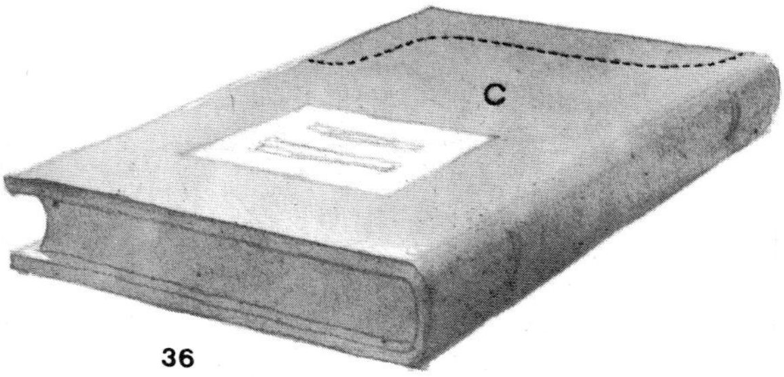

36

ed by the dotted line. Then clean the brush and spread this grey wash downwards, shading it. Finally, clean the brush again, dry it and wipe it on the rag (at this point you decide whether or not to suck it) and soak up the water and colour in the nearest section, which has to be lighter, blending the shading.

Now darken the edges a' and b' and the plane c' (the spine), painting on the same grey as before (or perhaps slightly darker) in another wash or coat which produces this darker tone. Using the same grey, paint the cast shadow, shading it along its outer edges (Fig. 37).

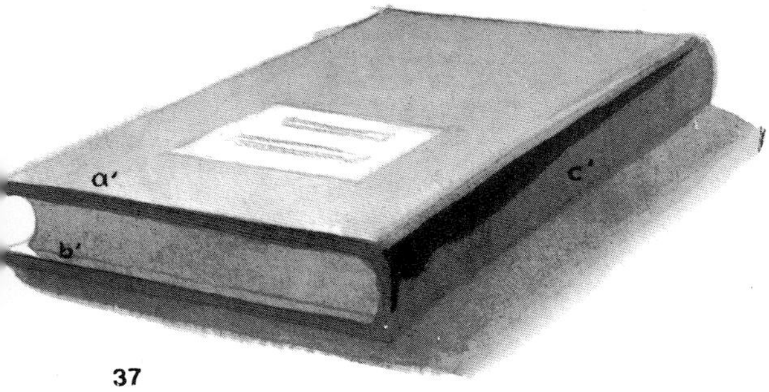

37

Finally, try to do the shading which gives us the «peak» shadow of the spine, that is the darkest part of that shadow. To see how, look at Fig. 37 and the finished picture in Fig. 38. Remember that first of all you have to paint a dark strip as shown in Fig. 37 and then, while it is still wet (quickly, please), shade this strip with a clean and almost dry brush — but with just a little water left — soaking it up and blending it until you get the picture shown in Fig. 38.

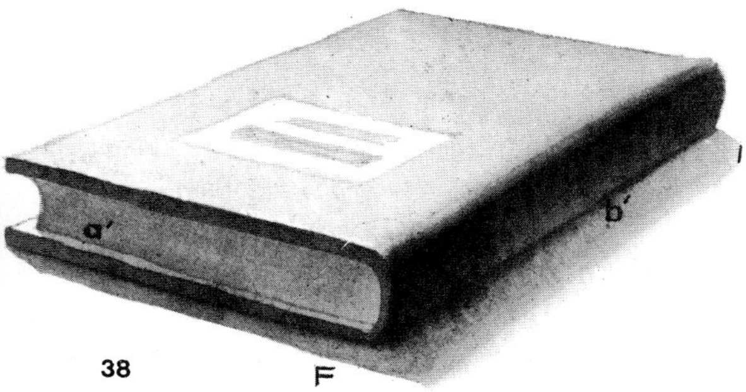

38

Two important points to remember:

1) for this or any other similar picture to be successful, the previous coat *must* be allowed to dry before adding another;

2) in this and similar cases, when the shading is not satisfactory or badly blended, it is best to wait until it is dry and repeat the operation.

To complete this exercise, darken the area marked b' with a dark line: paint the title of the book with a single brush-stroke and shade the area a' (the pages of the book) to bring out the plane formed by the cover.

EXERCISE B. MONOCHROME OF A CYLINDER AND A CUBE

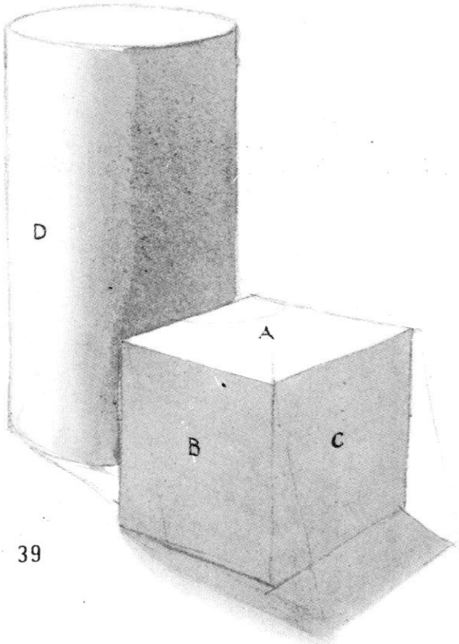

39

As before, very carefully draw the outline sketch producing the perspective effects and shadows of this picture.

Now begin by painting B and C of the cube with a grey wash, spreading the grey to the shadow cast by the cube. Again, as before, shade the edges of this shadow.

Now moisten the highlight side of the cylinder (D) with clean water, using the brush. When this area is wet, paint the grey producing the shadow of the cylinder. Shade this grey to the edge of the light area (Fig. 39). I would advise you here to turn the paper and work in this shading with horizontal strokes.

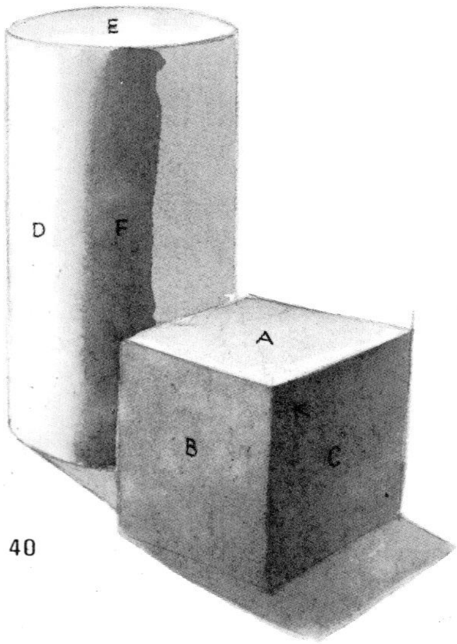

40

Darken the surface C of the cube, forming beads of wash along the left-hand upper edge (shown with an arrow) so that —by shading— this area is rather darker than the opposite one. Paint the shadow cast by the cylinder (on the ground behind the cube). Now do the smooth shading on surface A of the cube, painting from the furthest edge and shading towards the front (Fig. 40).

Paint the smooth shading on the top of the cylinder (E) (Fig. 40).

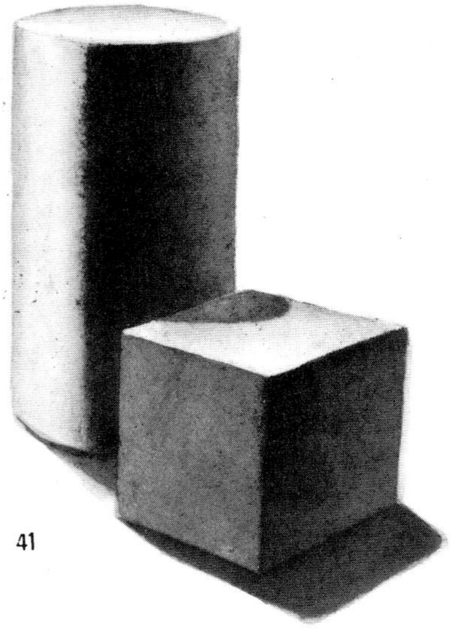

41

Finally, paint the shading for the cylinder's shadow. Begin by moistening the highlight D with clean water and apply a dark tone right along the edge, shading towards the right and spreading the tone towards the area in shadow. This should be done while this strip (F) is wet, working quickly to prevent «breaks», brushing from top to bottom and turning the paper so that you are painting in a horizontal direction. (Compare the shading of this section in Figs. 41 and 40).

Finish the picture by painting the shadow cast by the cylinder onto the cube.

EXERCISE C. MONOCHROME OF A SPHERE

First draw the sphere in pencil, using a compass if you like. Work out and draw in the shadow it casts. By means of a small circle mark the section of the sphere where the light would be brightest (G) so that throughout the exercise this area will be «reserved», that is ,will not be moistened nor painted.

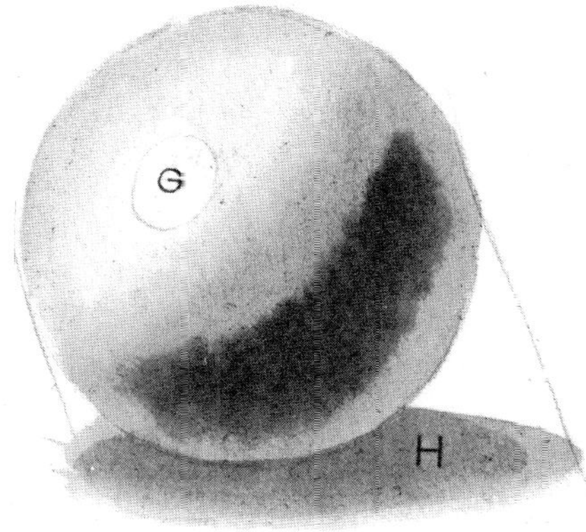

42

Begin by painting the shadowed section of the sphere, first moistening with a brush and clean water the illuminated section (without moistening the highlight G) and tinting all the illuminated area with a very light grey (the same used for making the previous shadow).

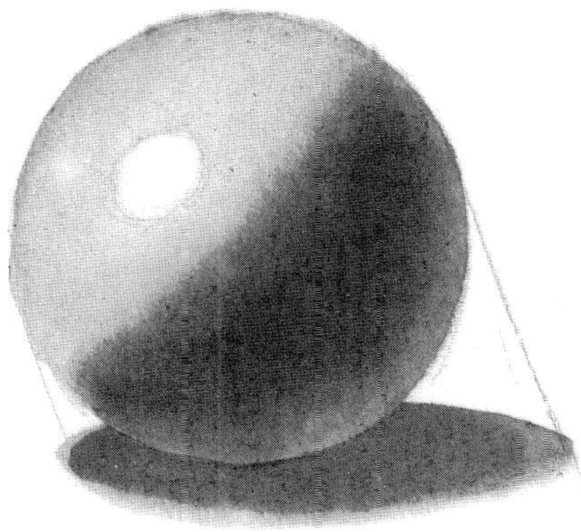
43

WAIT UNTIL THE FIRST WASH IS COMPLETELY DRY. Then moisten the shadowed area with a brush and clean water (not much water), «shading the water» up to the illuminated area. Paint a dark grey patch as shown in Fig. 42. If the area is sufficiently and evenly moist, the patch will spread of its own accord, avoiding the danger of «breaks». (Sorry, I forgot: before painting this patch, give it the tone of the shadow cast by the sphere (H). Wait until this shadow dries before continuing as above). Now work on the patch, shading it with an almost dry brush which in this case need not be cleaned (Fig. 43).

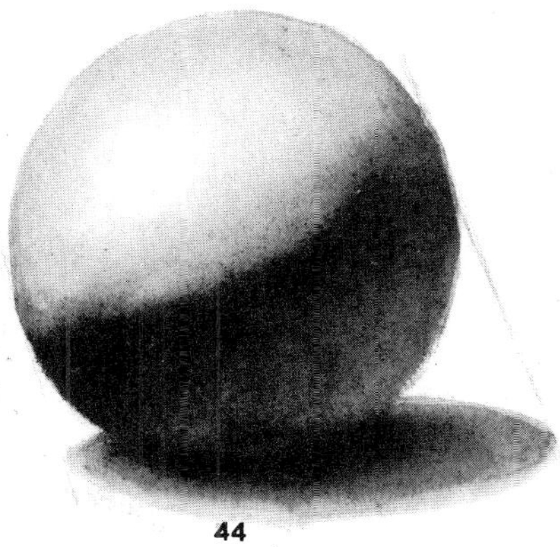
44

WAIT UNTIL IT DRIES before darkening. If the shading is not perfect, remember what I said earlier about waiting until it is dry before trying again.

And so on until you get the result shown in the model (Fig. 44). Remember that the section formed by the reflected light has to be painted by soaking up water and colour and that the circular shading of the illuminated area has to be obtained by painting a narrow strip along the edge of the sphere and shading it inwards to the high-light.

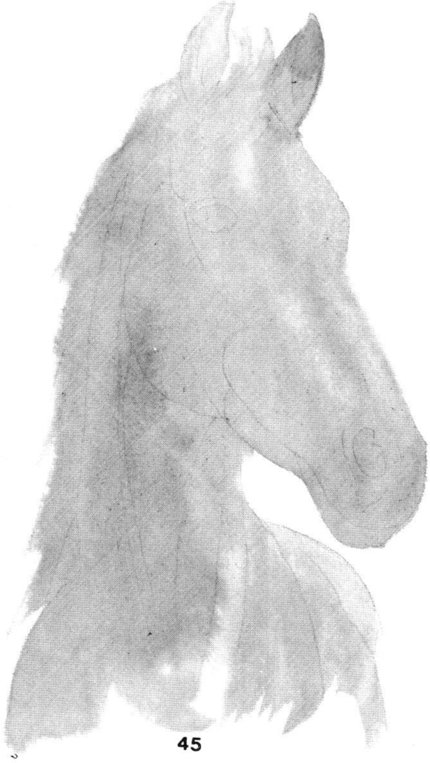

45

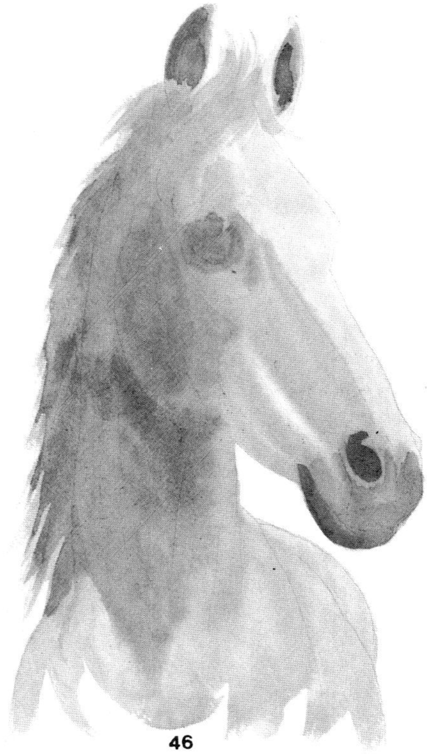

46

Exercise D. Monochrome of a horse's head

We shall now try to produce a monochrome of a horse's head, using as our model Fig. 49. To succeed in this exercise, it is absolutely essential to have practised and assimilated the practical exercises given earlier since the technique employed and the difficulties encountered are virtually the same.

We do not think it necessary to explain the exercise step by step since we feel that the knowledge already acquired will be enough to produce a satisfactory result.

INITIAL DRAWING

As always, you must begin with a very careful sketch, remembering that the final result depends to a great extent upon an accurate drawing. You can use the well-known method — frequently employed even by professional artists — of squaring up the model and reproducing this square on the drawing paper, either in the same size or enlarged by whatever method you find best. Briefly, then — and I must stress this — the essential point is to produce an absolutely accurate initial drawing.

FIRST STAGE: INITIAL TONING
MONOCHROME

Begin by wetting the entire picture of the horse's head, using a brush and clean water. Then paint a basic grey tone over it, a «wash» which — please remember — is intended right at the beginning to show as many as possible of the model's lightest tones (Fig. 45).

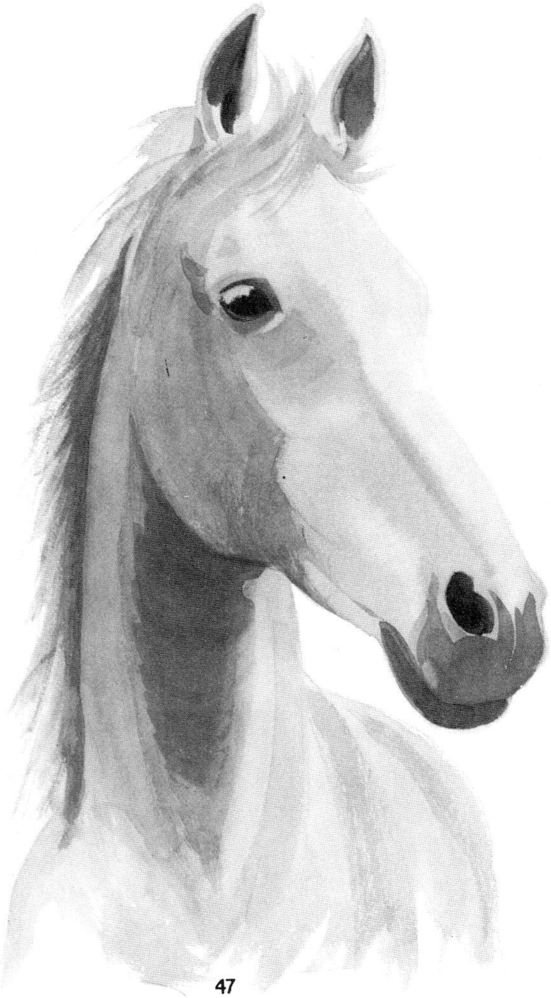
47

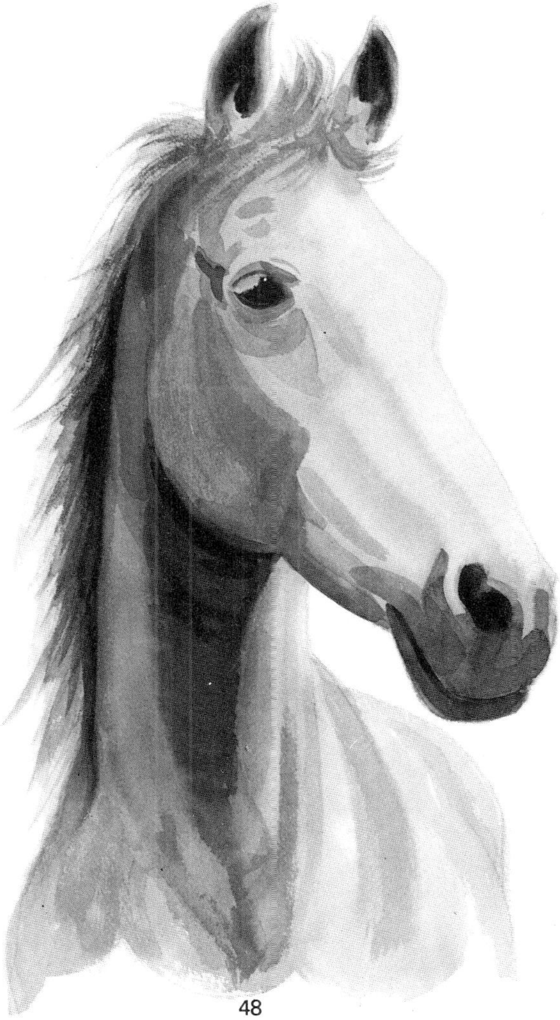
48

WITHOUT WAITING FOR THE PREVIOUS COAT TO DRY and working on the wet surface, apply another wash, picking out in advance the darkest values or tones of the model (Fig. 46).

NOW WAIT UNTIL THE PREVIOUS COATS ARE COMPLETELY DRY and work more thoroughly over the model until you obtain the result shown in Fig. 47.

SECOND STAGE: FINAL TONING

Still working on dry or wet surfaces, whichever is best, and applying all you have so far learnt about grey and shaded areas, continue to intensify the tonality until you reach the almost final stage shown in Fig. 48.

THIRD PHASE: FINAL TOUCHES

Last of all, look at Fig. 49, the finished work, remembering that it is produced only by patient and intelligent work, done without haste and obtained by constant comparison between the painting and the model

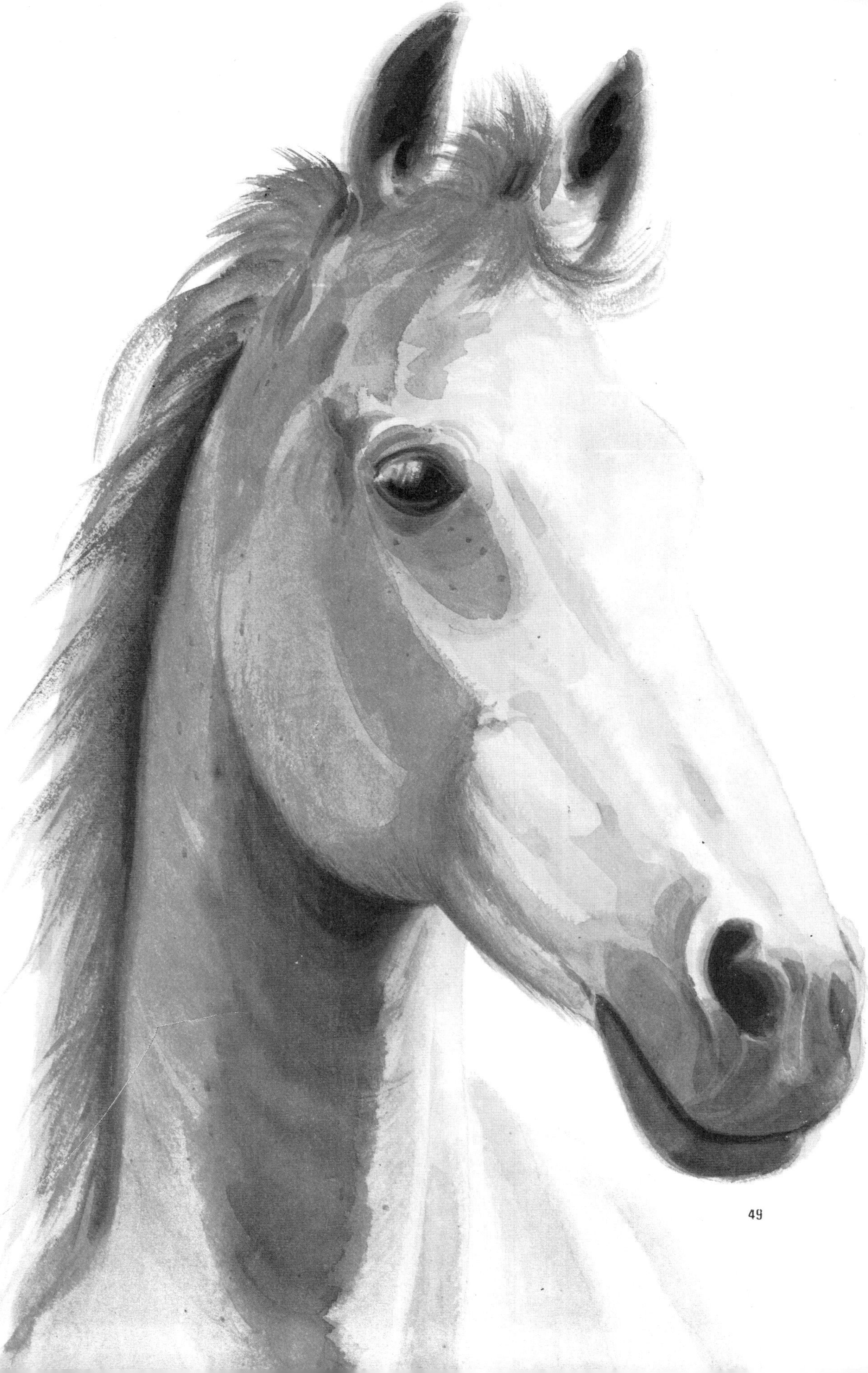

PAINTING WITH WATERCOLOUR (I)

DEFINITION OF WATERCOLOUR

Watercolour painting is the same as monochrome except that with the latter only one colour is used, while in watercolouring the artist works with every colour. So we can say:

Watercolour is a type of painting in which colours have been diluted to varying extents with water, applied to white paper, keeping the tones transparent and thus excluding the use of thick coats.

★

DESCRIPTION OF MATERIALS

Owing to the similarity between the process of monochrome and watercolour, we may in this list and examination of the materials used in watercolours repeat some of the ideas already explained in the previous chapter on monochrome.

Nevertheless, we think a description is needed both to amplify and stress what we have said before and to give a detailed account of the quality and use of the watercolour materials in the strict sense of the word which are here re-examined and analysed in keeping with the assessment and personal opinion of the artist Guillermo Fresquet.

BRUSHES

The brushes generally used for watercolours are sable and ichneumon, both being of good quality, while ichneumon is somewhat stiffer than sable. Cow's ear brushes may also be used although the quality is not so good as sable and ichneumon. To quote Guillermo Fresquet: «A good watercolour brush must have the following characteristics:

Qualities of a good brush

(1) The bristles must be fine and compact and they must bunch together perfectly when wet. (2) The brush must yield easily and respond smoothly to the pressure normally exerted by the artist's hand, and. 3) It must immediately recover its normal shape, that is to say the bunch of bristles must straighten out automatically when, after being wetted, pressure is no longer exerted» (Fig. 50).

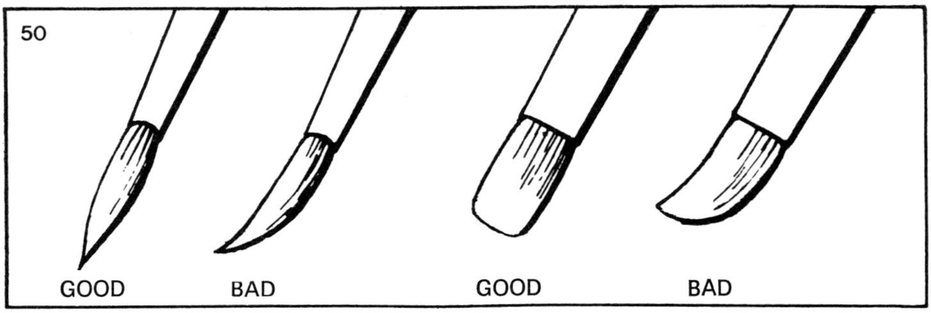

When painting watercolours for artistic purposes, it is not advisable to use fine brushes with a very low number since this may well condition the work, causing too many «finishing touches» and outlines of minor details. It is better to use a thick or sufficiently thick brush with a good «belly» (a large diameter through the centre of the bunch of bristles when the brush is loaded with water or watercolour) which permits rapid and spontaneous work. We should note here that if the brush is of good quality, it will have a perfect and compact point, even when thick and wet. There is no advantage, however, in having a wide range of brushes, since, in watercolour as in washpainting, the brush has to be continually washed in water to lighten or soak up colours, for merging shading, etc. Two round brushes, No. 8 and No. 10 (or No. 10 and No. 12) and one flat square-ended brush (No. 12 or 14) will be enough for every need.

Stock of brushes

Finally, for poster or commercial work (colour illustrations for a label, vignette, etc., a fine brush such as No. 2 or 4 is needed (Fig. 51).

Good class brushes are expensive, so it is essential to take good care of them. In particular, they should not be forgotten and left in the water-jar which, besides affecting the firmnes and flexibility, can dam-

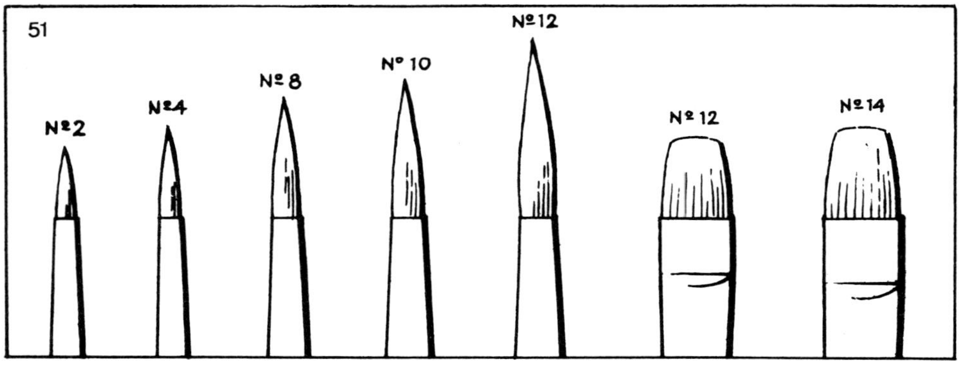

age the glue and the way the bristles are held in the ferrule of the brush. Moreover, the wooden handle may warp through too much water and affect the adjustment and firm hold of the metal ferrule. It is best to wash them thoroughly when the work is finished or when it is left over-

Care of brushes

night. The dry residue of colour is particularly damaging to the compact bunching of the bristles. After being washed in clean water, the brushes should be left in a large jar with the points upwards. If they are not to be used for some time, it is best to cover them with naphthalin to prevent their getting dusty.

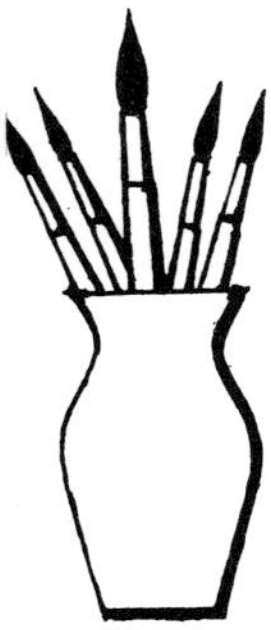

52

WATERCOLOURS

Composition of watercolours

Watercolours are made of vegetable, animal or mineral pigments — basically those used for making up oils — agglutinated with water and gum arabic to which are added other ingredients such as glycerine, honey and a preserving agent. Glycerine and honey are used to make the gum arabic malleable, preventing splits after rather thick coats have been put on. In their final form, the colours are pastes which are packed in tin tubes or shaped into solid blocks or pastilles and arranged in small pans or white plastic or metal cups.

Packing and brands

It is rare nowadays for the artist to prepare his own colours, since there are several good firms which produce and sell excellent watercolours. Here we can mention the foreign brands, Rembrandt, Talens, Watteau, Paillard, Pelikan, Schmincker, etc. In Britain, there are, among others, Reeves, Windsor and Newton and Rowneys.

Most of these firms manufacture their colours in both tubes and pastilles, producing a range which can include up to fifty or sixty different colours. This astonishing variety is due to the fact that in many cases — as in oil painting — professional watercolour artists prefer to choose their own stock. However, the manufacturers generally offer tubes or pastilles in metal boxes which contain the range of colours previously chosen. Boxes of 6, 8, 10, 12 and up to 24 colours are available and when they are used up, individual tubes or pastilles can be obtained as replacements.

Tubes or pastilles?

This brings us to the question of whether it is better to use tubes or pastilles, that is to say, which of the two methods is most suitable: colour in the form of paste packed in tubes or solid colour in blocks or pastilles.

There is no firm criterion, but watercolour in tubes, being in the form of paste which is quickly dissolved in water, seems to make the professional artist's job easier and in many cases induces spontaneous and lively work... this does not mean, however, that those using blocks or pastilles are not skilful too. Of course, when working with solid pastilles, they must be of good quality and have the maximum solubility — they must quickly dissolve and produce pigmentation when the brush, loaded with water, is applied to the pastille. For the pigments to be easily soluble, the pastilles must be «fresh» and recently manufactured.

Watercolours most commonly used by the professional artist:

Lemon yellow
Golden yellow
Yellow ochre
Burnt sienna
Vermilion
Carmine
Viridian
Cobalt blue
Ultramarine blue
Black

Besides these colours, some boxes contain white, usually in a tube. The French brand Paillard, for example, includes a tube of Permanent White in its boxes. This seems contrary to the general rule that white must not be used in watercolour. We hasten to add that besides the «transparent white», white is included in the range as an auxiliary for other colours (for instance, to obtain a specific shade of grey by adding black). It should be noted, moreover, that while the use of white as a direct colour is «forbidden» in watercolour technique, professional artists accept that white can be employed as mentioned above for very thin white lines: lines which represent ships' rigging painted on a blue sky, short or thin light branches on a dark background, etc.

White in watercolour

PALETTES

Boxes of watercolours now serve both to contain the colours and as a palette or utensil in which the colours are made up or mixed. This latter function, which is so necessary when the artist is painting away from his studio, for instance, when doing a landscape in the open, has induced the manufacturers to make the boxes in metal, painted or enamelled white inside with the cover shaped as a number of hollows which, acting as cups or small containers, we can fill with small amounts of water for preparing watercolours, for preparing mixtures of thicker colours, for testing the intensity and tonality of a colour, etc. Carrying this idea further, some boxes not only include these hollows in the cover but also in the box itself. Paillard, for instance, sells its colours in a box with a double bottom, packing the colours in a metal container which, when taken out of the box, is transformed into a large palette with hollows in the cover and bottom (See Fig. 59, page 41).

Watercolour boxes used as palettes

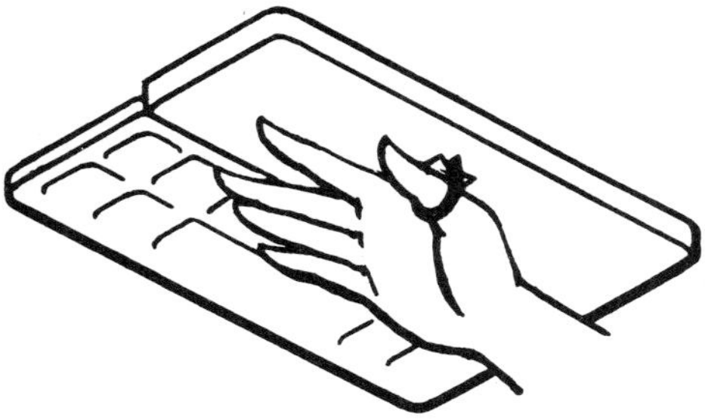

53

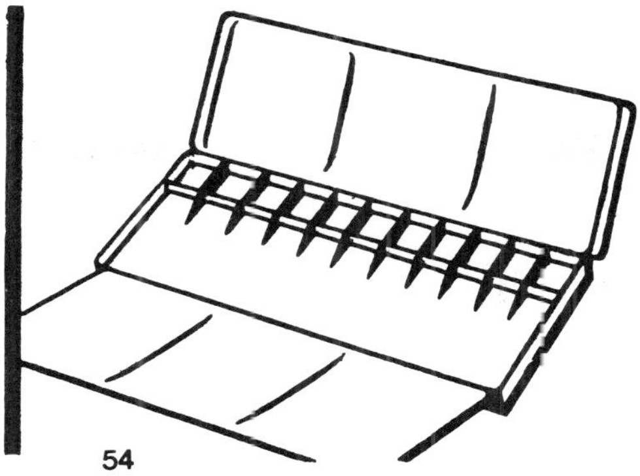

54

Finally, to improve their use as palettes, all modern boxes have a special ring on their underside in which the painter can insert his thumb and hold it in the position normally used for oil-painting, using the hand holding his brushes (Fig. 53).

As well as the palette-type box described above, palettes specially designed for watercolour are available. Most of them are metal and somewhat larger than the traditional oval or rectangular type but similar to those used for oils. There is also a special model very popular with professional watercolour painters: this is a real palette-box designed for painting with watercolours in tubes and consisting of two or three separate units in the form of a folding case. One of these units has a series of compartments of small square cavities in which the colour is placed when squeezed from the tube. The rest of the case is divided into smooth hollows similar to those found in ordinary boxes. Left-over paint can be left in the compartments for use at subsequent sessions. If they are to be used later, separate compartments must of course be kept for each colour, so that the one reserved for cobalt blue, for instance, is always used for and replenished with that colour (Fig. 54).

Special palettes for painting with watercolour

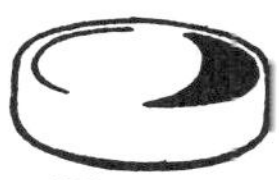

55

When working in a studio, a professional artist may well use an ordinary china plate as a palette, placing the colours around its edge — using colours from a tube — and mixing them in the centre. Individual cups are also commonly used in studio work: these are made of china or plastic with one or several cavities (Figs 55, 56 and 57).

56

Finally, we must mention that when working on small paintings in their studio, many professional artists use an ordinary piece of paper on which the mixtures are made up and the colours tested: the brushes are also rubbed on them to form the point or unload water, etc.

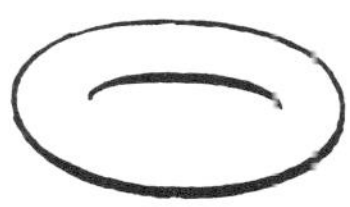

57

Whatever type is used, the colours should be arranged and kept in one order, and always placed and mixed in the same area: this makes the work easier and produces purer mixtures of colours. The following order can be used:

ORDER OF COLOURS ON THE PALETTE

From right to left:

White
Lemon yellow (or medium cadmium)
Golden yellow (or orange yellow)
Yellow ochre
Burnt sienna
Vermilion
Carmine
Emeraude green
Cobalt blue
Ultramarine blue
Black

Notice how the light colours are separated from the dark, white from black, yellow from blue, etc., while at the same time an attempt is made to arrange the subsidiary shades between them: yellow and ochre, vermilion and carmine, etc.

RAGS, SPONGES AND BLOTTERS

When you are busy painting, all you need for drying and soaking up surplus water from the brush is a piece of clean rag.

A piece of clean rag; a small sponge or, otherwise, a flat brush.

Some artists also use a small sponge with its end attached to an old brush handle. This is used for washing the paper with clean water before painting, for soaking up water and colour from a moist area or for putting in special textural effects and finishing touches. Guillermo Fresquet prefers to do all these jobs with a flat brush such as that described earlier.

When working in his studio, the professional artist sometimes grabs some white blotting-paper which is better than nothing when trying to obtain textural effects, soaking up water and colour, making «breaks», etc.

WATER-JARS

Fresh water is used for watercolours and placed in two jars, one for the first wash of the brushes and the other for the second. You can buy special jars for this, which have two small lips inserted in the upper edge for holding the brush (Fig. 58). But, as we said in the section on monochrome, a glass jam-jar is perfectly suitable if it is large enough to prevent the water becoming dirty after the first few washes.

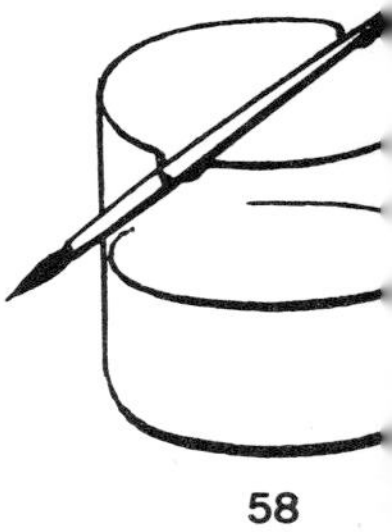

58

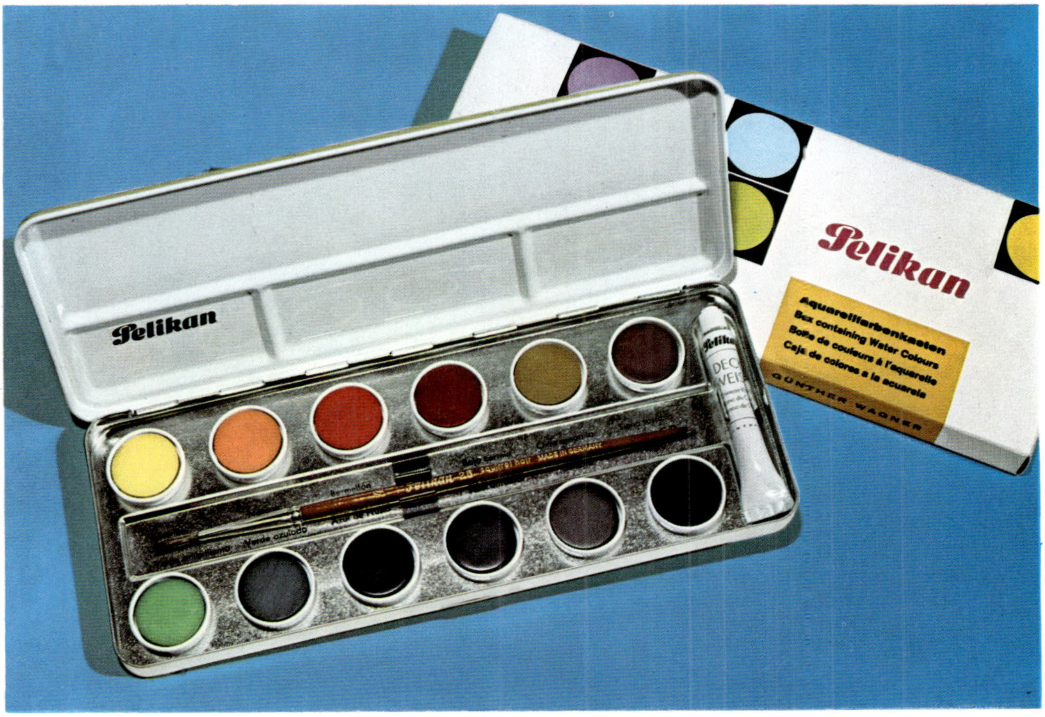

59

These jars or containers are only used for studio work. When painting out of doors there are other types which we shall discuss later.

PAPER FOR WATERCOLOUR

Watercolours must be painted on white paper. The type and quality of the paper are extremely important. Generally speaking, any good quality heavy paper with good priming and texture is suitable for watercolours. We can explain these features in more detail:

Characteristics of paper for use in watercolouring

Paper for use in watercolours must be very carefully manufactured and have adequate priming. The quality depends upon the raw material used, which in the case of first-class drawing-paper consists of pieces of linen processed into a very fine paste. Handwoven or vat paper is produced by laying a thin coat of this wet paste on a fine metal screen which allows the surplus liquid to drain off. The sheet then undergoes a number of processes, including priming. For our purpose the amount of glue used determines the extent to which the moisture is absorbed when the watercolour is applied. If no glue at all is used, the colour will spread just like a drop of water on blotting-paper: too much glue will make the paper waterproof, which means that the colour will take a long time to dry, causing «breaks» and uneven washes.

Ideally, the amount of glue used should enable the watercolour to dry comparatively quickly while allowing time for soaking up with the brush —producing whites and light colours— for changing colour while it is still wet, etc. but without making the painter wait too long for it to dry, which has a bad effect upon the spontaneity of the work.

The paper must be rough with a clearly visible grain, enabling washes to be added without producing «breaks» and also forming a kind of sediment in the minute cavities of the grain which is a distinctive feature of watercolours. It should be emphasized that papers which are completely smooth or have only a very fine grain are unsuitable for watercolours.

The paper must have a grain.

The grain in the paper is a decisive factor when it comes to touching up and finishing-off the work. A thick grain is usually advisable for large pictures covering the entire sheet, where the grainy appearance caused by the sediment and darker colours in the channels of the paper favours the production of a large-scale subject with extensive patches of colour with the brush being used as a swab, in fact a conception closer to impressionism. On the other hand, finely-grained paper favours the blending of the washes, producing a more delicately finished appearance, suitable for small paintings and also for watercolours for use in advertising, book illustration, vignettes or commercial art.

Various uses for paper according to the grain.

As a final feature, watercolour paper must be sufficiently thick not to wrinkle or cockle when wet. (Guillermo Fresquet rightly claims that such wrinkles or cockles are sometimes an insurmountable problem not only for an amateur but even for a professional artist. We must remember the method of mounting and stretching the paper to prevent loss of shape caused by the moisture in the water as described earlier when we discussed monochromes. «A temporary means of overcoming this problem,» Fresquet says, «is to moisten the paper by wetting it with a brush and a little water and then fixing it to the drawing board with eight or so drawing-pins. You will find that when it is dry, it is comparatively taut.»)

The problem of wrinkling caused by moisture.

You can buy several brands of good paper which have the characteristics described above: I can mention the foreign makes produced by Canson of «Canson & Montgolfier», the English make, Whatman, the Germans, Turm, Universal, Schoellersten, etc. and the Spanish Guarro, which specialises in drawing-paper. Watercolour paper is commonly called torchon-paper. All these firms provide papers of different thickness and various degrees of grain. In most cases the brand is identifiable by a water-mark —as the experts call it— showing the surface of the paper to be used.

Good brands of water-colour paper.

Watercolour paper mounted on cardboard is also used, which, besides overcoming the problem of wrinkling and the cockles caused by moisture, also provides a drawing-board or support.

As we said in the section on monochrome, it is sensible to try various qualities and types of paper until you find which is most suitable for your skill or speciality and then continue to use that one.

SUPPORTS

When working in his studio, Guillermo Fresquet generally uses a

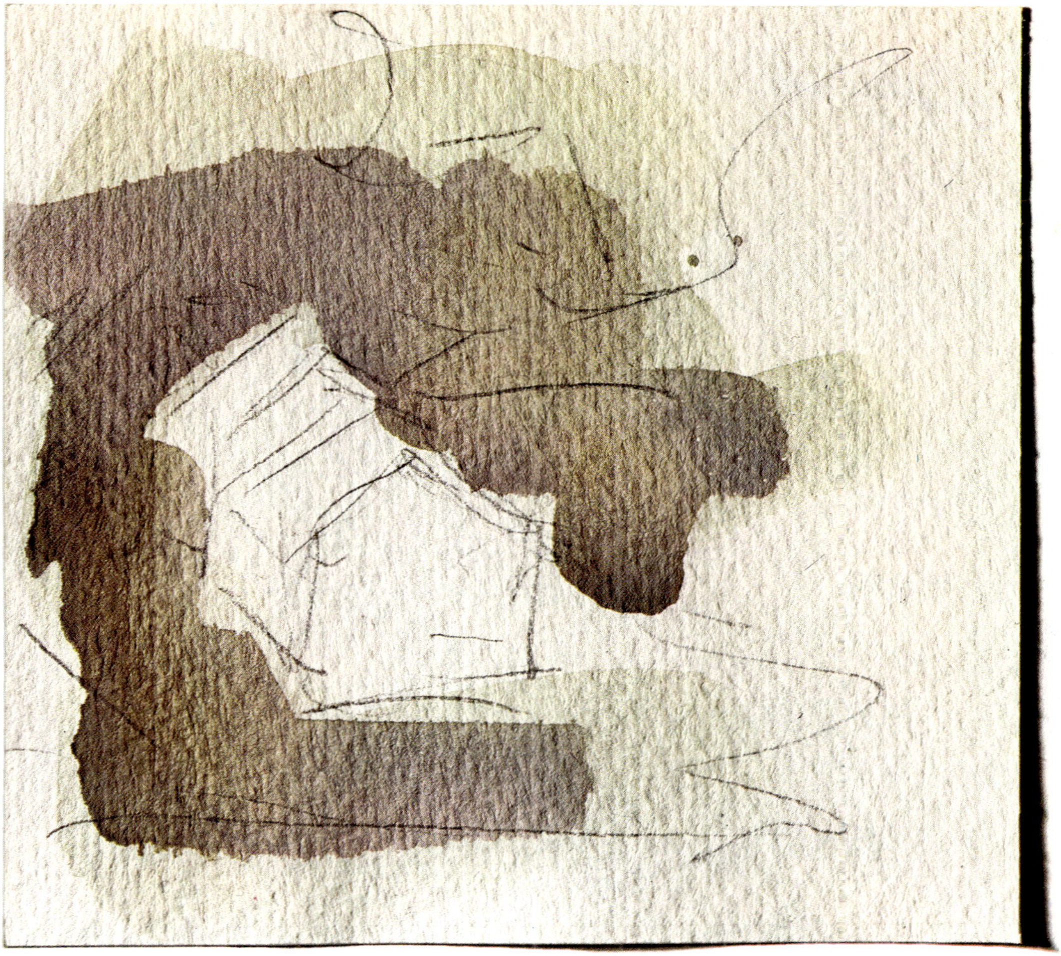

60. This is a sample of the paper used for watercolour painting.

ving-
d or
r as
port.

portfolio cover or wooden board, depending upon what is available. When using a wooden board, he fastens the paper with drawing-pins and, whith a portfolio cover, he uses metal clips. In either case, he rests it upon the drawing-table and his lap, tilting the support according to the job he is doing and the effects he is trying to obtain by using varying amounts of water and colour.

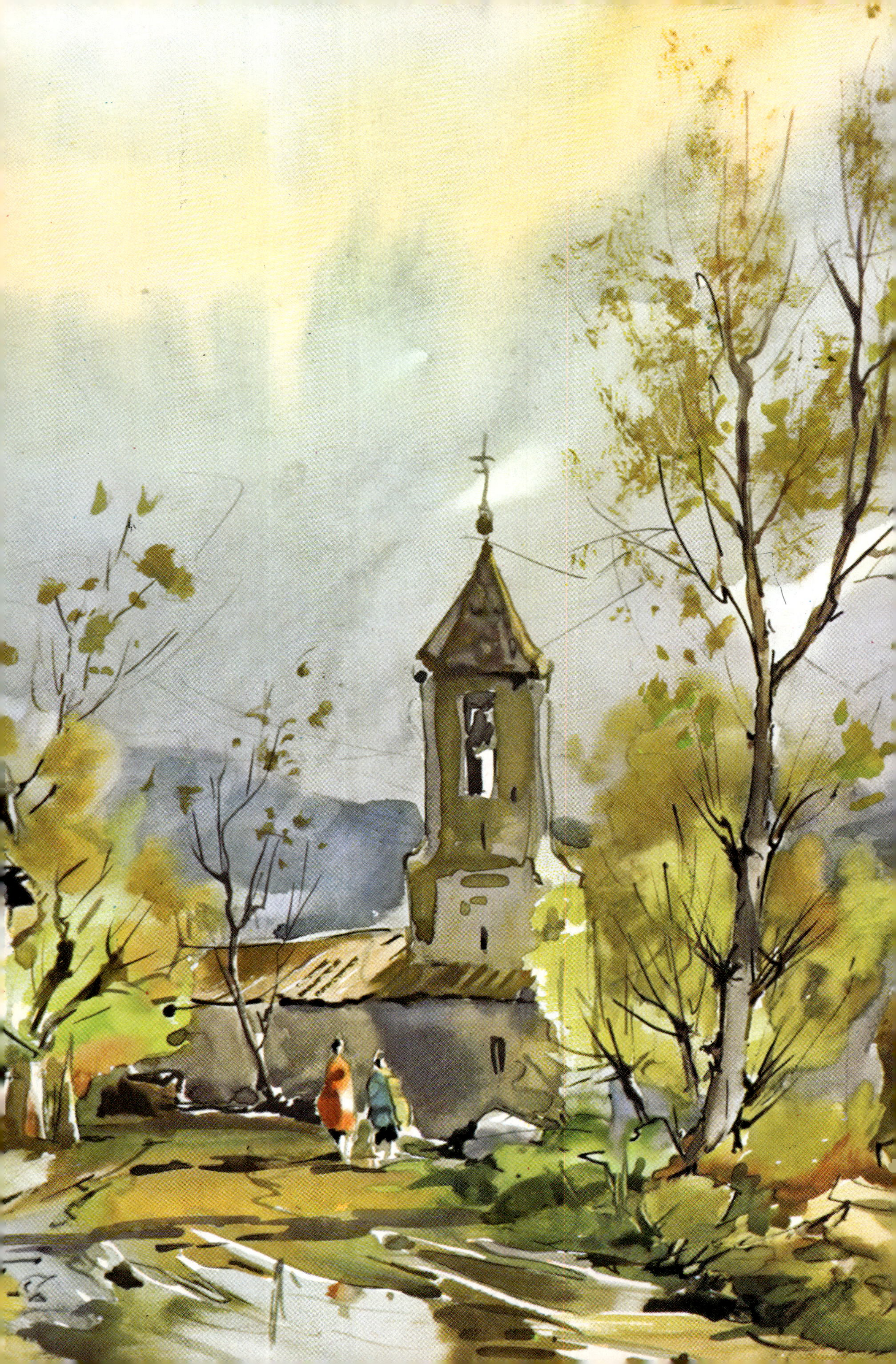

The materials described in the previous paragraphs have, of course, to be supplemented with some special pot when the artist works out of doors in order to paint an urban scene, a seascape, harbour scene or a landscape. It is not practical to go into the country with a glass water-jar.

So, here is a list and description of these special containers:

SPECIAL EQUIPMENT FOR PAINTING OUT OF DOORS

We must mention before anything else that it is perfectly possible to paint out of doors with the equipment described above without having to obtain special items. In our enthusiasm, all we professionals have at some time or another gone off to paint a watercolour with just an ordinary portfolio under our arms, a box of watercolours, a glass bottle and an aluminium jar, nothing else, no easel, no stool, looking for a place in the shade, a tree-trunk or stone to sit on and a stream or tap for filling our bottle and jar. («And how we used to enjoy ourselves» adds Fresquet).

But, let's face it; times have changed and «la vie bohême», inconvenience and privations are not suited to modern times. Briefly, this is what you need:

A box for your colours

Special boxes for holding the watercolour materials.

If you paint with solid pastilles, their metal box, with the top divided into compartments for mixing and compounding the colours and ring underneath to enable you to hold it like a palette, is all you need. So we can say that pastilles are better than tubes.

If you paint with tubes, a small wooden box or case will be required. You can buy some which are specially designed to take the colours, palette, brushes, rags, etc., as well as metal container for the water.

Palette

Palette

When painting from tubes it is essential to have a palette. This may be the traditional type similar to those used for oils, or the special kind described above.

Brush container

Keeping the brushes in good condition.

You may obtain a special leather or plastic pouch for brushes, keeping the points and bristles in good condition. Or you can easily use two cardboard boxes, one containing a couple of rubber bands for holding the brushes.

Water containers

Special water containers.

You will find that shops specialising in artists' materials will have various kinds of metal containers, flat and long, with a screw-top, for holding a sufficient amount of water for outdoor painting. You will also need a plastic or aluminium jar.

PORTFOLIO

Even if you use an easel, a portfolio is necessary for carrying and holding watercolour paper, apart from its usefulness for carrying the completed watercolour.

Portofolio for holding the paper.

As we have said, this portfolio may save you the expense of buying an easel for outdoor work.

OUTDOOR EASEL

Folding easels, specially designed for watercolour painting, are available. Some of them also have a fitted box. However, it is perfectly possible — and common practice — to use an outdoor oil-painting easel which has been adapted for watercolours. In most cases, adapting it consists simply of attaching the portfolio and watercolour paper instead of the canvas for oil-painting.

A special easel or one used for oils.

STOOL

Finally, to complete the list, we must remember a folding stool so that we can sit down wherever we want. These are made of wood, with a canvas seat and wooden legs or of metal throughout to suit all tastes and weights, as you can see in Fig. 62.

Stools

THE POTENTIAL OF WATERCOLOUR

As an artistic medium, watercolour can be placed second to the premier form of painting: oils. That it can be used for a virtually unlimited range of subjects is proved by the fact that museums and famous collections all over the world possess watercolours of landscapes, figures, portraits and examples of still-life. However, natural subjects for watercolour are undoubtedly landscapes, especially country or urban scenes, and seascapes. Rocky scenes with a few old houses, country or characteristic streets or squares, a view of escarpments or boats at anchor, harbour scenes, railway or industrial scenes, all these are suitable watercolour subjects, both on account of their natural beauty and because they include human activities which are generally the artist's prime consideration. Don't imagine, however, that watercolour must always confine itself to preconceived subjects, typical scenes or rustic landscapes. The drama of a cloudy afternoon in the country, a flat, barren countryside, wild as a Highland moor, can be suggested as a subject. So can a view of an airport, with a low horizon and enormous grey cloudy sky which becomes a protagonist itself in view of the subject. These can be extremely effective and witness to a high artistic standard linked with a new conception of the medium.

Possible subjects.

Watercolour is also used by artists as an ideal medium for small preliminary studies for large oil-paintings or pictures which are to be used as murals painted in oils or tempera or as frescoes.

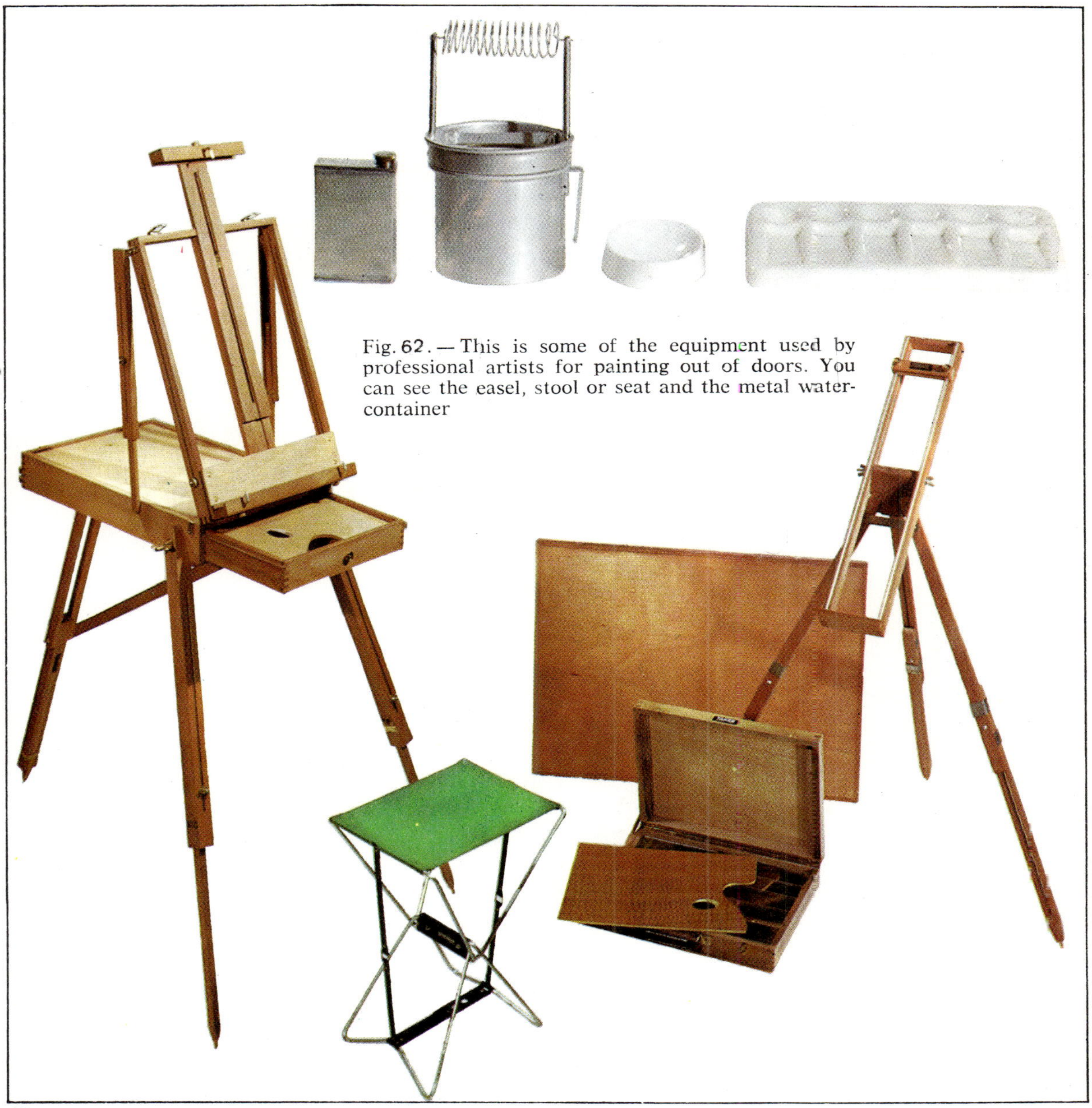

Fig. 62. — This is some of the equipment used by professional artists for painting out of doors. You can see the easel, stool or seat and the metal water-container

62

We must also mention the use of watercolour as a medium employed in architecture and interior decoration for making the initial perspective drawings for buildings, shops and interiors in general, as well as for designing machinery, equipment and other objects.

In commercial art, watercolour is one of the most commonly used media both for drafting out posters, etc. and for book illustrations, colour advertisements, brochures and vignettes for use in pamphlets, labels and so on.

Watercolour in commercial art.

Watercolour is also an ideal medium for painting pictures for children's books: fairy tales, encyclopaedias, school primers, etc. It is also suitable for cartoon and advertising films both for the figure studies and the backgrounds.

The only restriction placed upon watercolour is the size used. It is not fit for large pictures or decorative panels which exceed the standard size of a sheet of watercolour paper (47 x 68 or 52 x 65 cm. which in itself is fairly big). It is customary to paint to the size of a medium sheet: 34 x 47 cm. or 32 x 52 cm.

Sizes commonly used by artists.

The sizes normally used for watercolours:

34 x 47 cm or 32 x 52 cm

In commercial art there is, of course, no standard size. The original or final picture is always painted the same size as the block or up to half as large again, retaining the correct proportions. For example, a block measuring 14 x 20 cm may be painted the same size or quarter (17.5 x 25 cm) or even half (21 x 30 cm) up. When reduced to the original size by the photo-engraver, these proportionally larger paintings provide a better printed illustration.

Size used in commercial art.

THEORY, TECHNIQUE AND SKILL OF WATERCOLOUR PAINTING

When comparing an oil-painting with a watercolour, even the least knowledgeable realise that in the oil-painting the paint is thick, forming a thick coat from which the covering quality of the medium can be appreciated, while in the watercolour the coats of colour are thin, invisible, transparent and do no more than darken the paper. This transparency is one of the main features of watercolour. It is produced simply because the colours are weakened or lightened with water instead of white paint. For instance, in order to paint a rose colour in oil, the artist mixes red and white paint together and obtains a thick rose with which he can over-paint and even cover a darker colour. With watercolour this rose has to be produced from red colour and water, weakening the red and lightening it with water while allowing for the fact that

With watercolours, the paper regulates the tone and intensity of the colour.

the white of the paper will show through the thin red coat. So with watercolour the white of the paper regulates the tone and intensity of the colour — it plays the same part as white oil-paint. A small amount of red with a large amount of water will allow the paper to show a considerable degree of white, producing a pale rose. If the amount of red is increased, there will be less transparency and the white of the paper will be less evident, producing a bright rose colour. Finally, when the red is applied with only a little water, the coat of paint will cover the white of the paper, producing a strong red, even if the coat is only a very thin film.

If the main feature of watercolour is its transparency, what does this mean in practice?

Firstly: When painting with watercolour it is impossible to superimpose a light colour on a dark colour

Let's go back to oil. Imagine that you are painting a purple with oils. Could you paint a light yellow over it? Of course you could. You may have to wait until the purple coat is dry — or perhaps not, it all depends — but you would certainly find no difficulty in painting a light yellow over it. To obtain a light yellow with watercolour, on the other hand, you would have to dilute a small amount of yellow with water, producing a wash whose colour is incapable of overcoming and covering the intensity of the first purple coat.

Secondly: When painting with watercolour it is necessary to work upwards and outwards

If it is impossible to paint light colours over dark, there is, of course, no other way but to paint upwards and outwards, that is to say gradually intensifying the tone and colour, remembering for instance that we shall always be able to darken a light blue by superimposing another coat of blue and transforming it into a darker blue. Which brings us to the third factor:

Thirdly: When painting with watercolour, the white and light coloured areas must be marked out in advance

If, in this landscape we are painting, there is a white cottage surrounded by trees and thickets, we must first paint the green of the bushes and trees, leaving out the white area of the house If a light earth-coloured lane runs beside the house, the light sienna of this area will

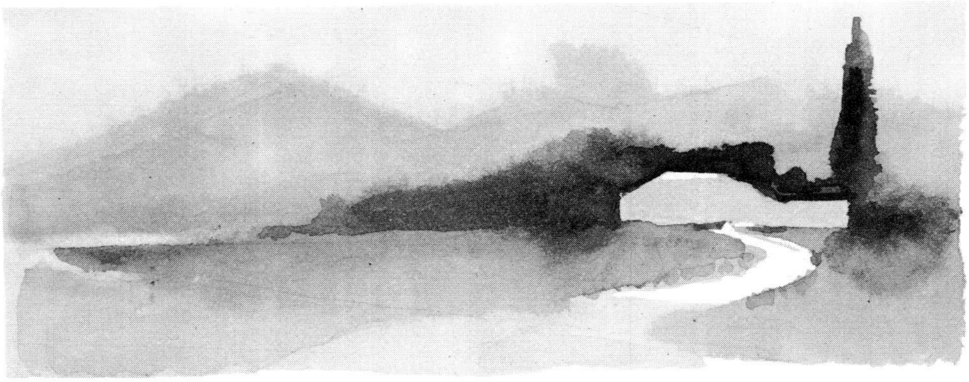

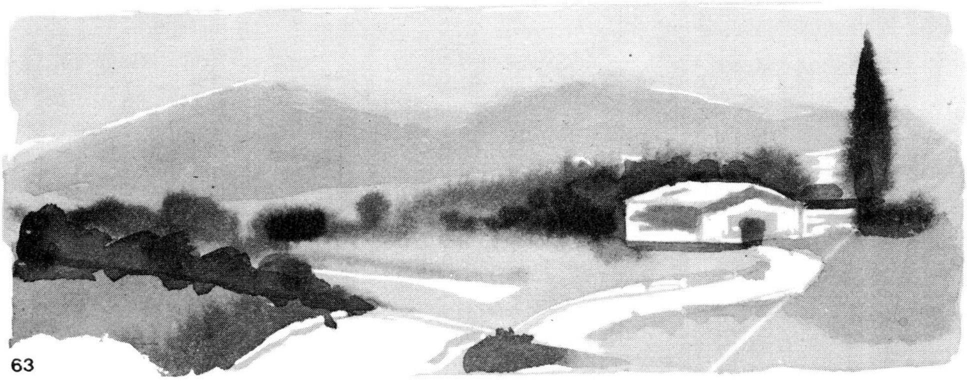

63

have to be painted first — or afterwards if we first mark out the shape of the lane — then superimposing the dark sienna bordering it, i.e. working upwards and outwards. It is then possible to emphasize it with another coat, intensifying the colour of the lane and its edges (Fig. 63).

But this involves no difficulties. Being able to intensify tones by applying further coats of colour means that we can in some cases change or blend colours. Imagine, for instance, that you have painted a green field. Suppose that after you have put on the first coat you find that the green is too yellow. All you need do is to apply another coat of bluish green or sky blue which makes the previous green turn bluish, losing its yellow tint. This field may also contain a tree or some darker green bushes with a reddish tinge, that is a burnt green, a brownish green or simply a khaki. All you need do then is to paint a reddish green or even a dark rose over the pure green, and with the colour of the first coat coming through and combining with the transparency of the second you will obtain the shade you want.

Changing colours by superimposing further coats.

This feature of watercolour (always produced by painting upwards and outwards, with dark colours on light colours) reminds us that colours can be obtained by superimposing or mixing in others. Let me begin by stressing that:

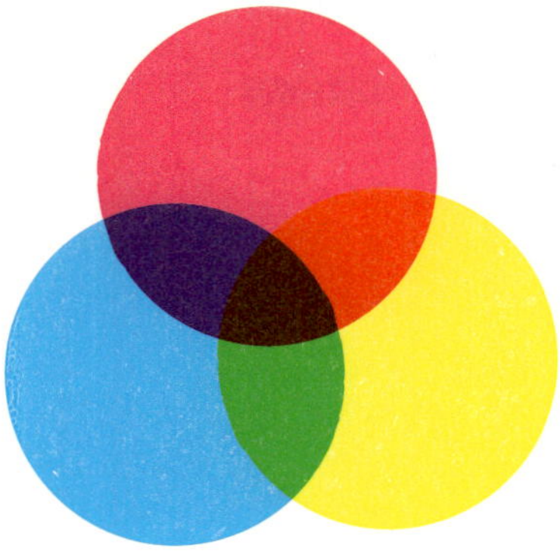

64

With just the three primary colours

CYANINE (OR PRUSSIAN) BLUE,
PURPLE (OR CARMINE)
YELLOW

it is possible to obtain all the colours of nature, including black. (Fig. 64).

Colour theory

Excuse me for stressing this but, as you already know, if two of these three primary colours are mixed together, they produce three new «secondary» colours. When mixed with the primaries, these in turn provide us with six tertiary colours. If we then mix the primaries and secondaries with the tertiaries, we obtain twelve quaternaries, and so on until we have an infinite range of colours. Do you remember? (Fig. 65).

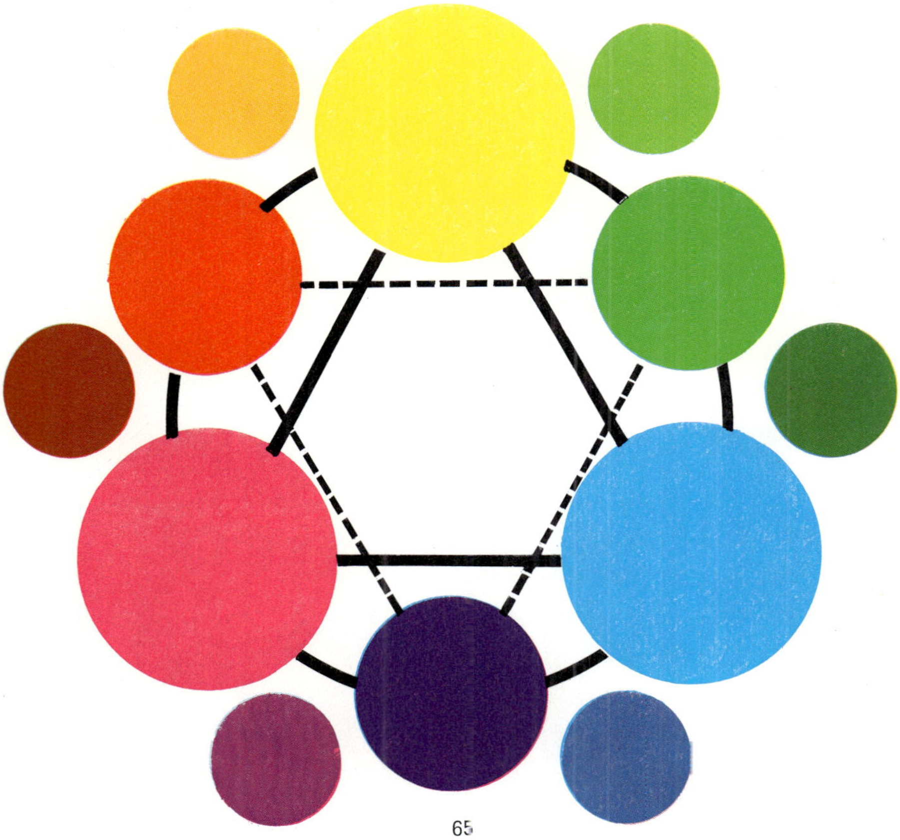

65

PRIMARIES	+	PRIMARIES	=	SECONDARIES
Purple	+	yellow	=	red
Yellow	+	cyanine blue	=	green
Cyanine blue	+	purple	=	dark violet-blue

PRIMARIES	+	SECONDARIES	=	TERTIARIES
Yellow	+	green	=	light green
Green	+	cynanine blue	=	viridian
Dark blue	+	cynanine blue	=	ultramarine blue
Dark blue	+	purple	=	violet
Purple	+	red	=	carmine
Red	+	yellow	=	orange

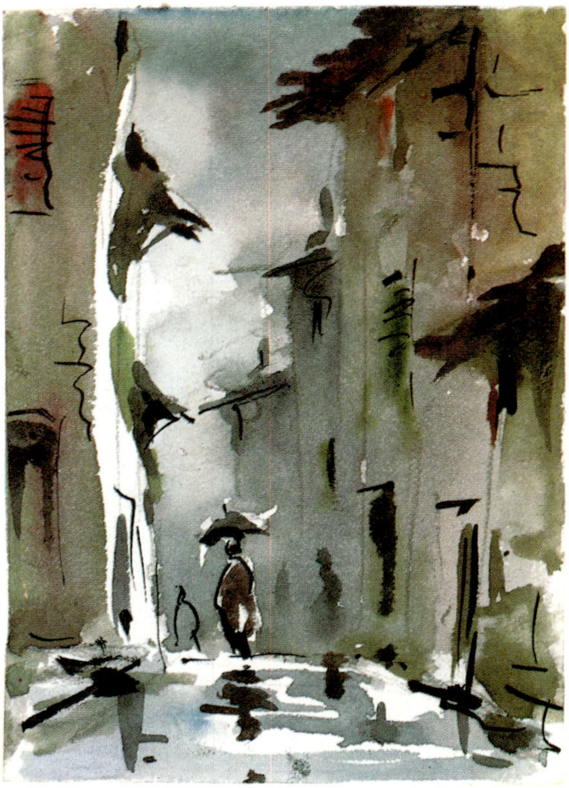
66

In this superb sketch Guillermo Fresquet has given us an example of the technique and potential of «wet watercolours», a method based upon applying colour on wet paper or coats, producing the atmosphere of this picture.

In the next chapter we shall study in detail the method used for painting this type of watercolour, including a number of exercises formulated and illustrated by the painter of this sketch.

We have described the theory and principles of watercolours. Now we shall deal with the theory and all the «tricks of the trade» which can amend some of these principles for instance, the rule that you must paint upwards and outwards or that with watercolours, the whites and light colours must be marked out in advance.

Don't worry, we are not going to contradict ourselves. In principle, the rules remain valid: you should paint upwards and outwards, gradually darkening the tones and colours, and you should at the very beginning mark out the white and light colours. But...

THE INTRINSIC FEATURE OF WATERCOLOUR: RAPID WORKING

When using watercolours, in the current sense of the word, it is impossible to plan to paint a picture in several sessions. The detailed approach and finicky work of some masters of the last century may have compelled them to stop half-way and leave it until the next day owing to lack of time but this is not done with the current style of watercolours.

Modern watercolour must be considered a painting of an impression

All modern artists and books on the subject say that watercolour must be considered as the painted expression of an impression, a work which captures a landscape in a moment for just as long as it takes to paint «that sunlight, those colours, those effects of light and shade». Under these circumstances, the artist's attitude can only resemble a kind of trance, rather like a fever which affects all his faculties: his sense of the proportions and dimensions, his memory of forms, his perception of colour, his ability to see it, draw it and paint it all at the same time. No more than two hours should be needed to paint a landscape in watercolour. Let me repeat this:

About two hours is the maximum time required for painting a landscape in watercolours.

It may not be too much to claim that such rapid conception and execution is the indirect reason for the «wet» style which is greatly esteemed and practised by many modern artists.

THE «WET WATERCOLOUR» STYLE

Method for «wet watercolour»

You first moisten the paper with clean water and, without waiting for it to dry, paint a green field, for instance, in the foreground and, again without waiting for it to dry, put in a range of mountains in the background. Using the moisture, add a darker green over the first green, painting a strip of trees and blades of grass... continue in this way, now and again soaking up the water to delineate shapes or to make contrasts,

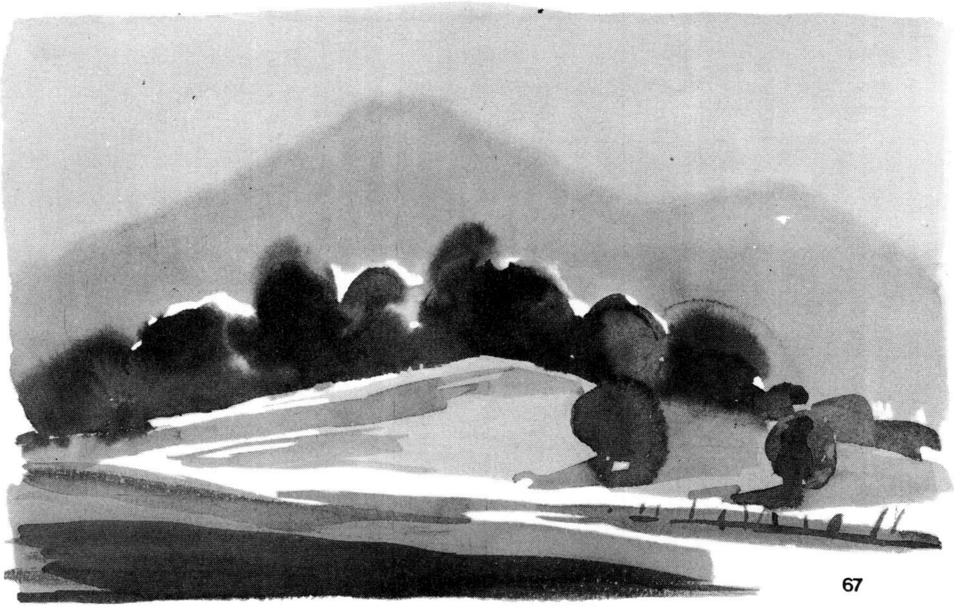

67

at other times adding colour... you are now painting in «wet watercolour», obtaining a special style where the shapes have a particular atmosphere, without firm outlines, particularly the distant profiles and masses (Fig. 67).

(The effects produced by wet watercolour are particularly useful for subjects with little contrast such as grey landscapes without sun, cloudy scenes, rainy days, etc. The technique of wet watercolours is also usually suitable for backgrounds, clouds, etc. even when the subject contains wide contrasts, for instance, a sunny landscape).

«PAINTING» LIGHT COLOURS ON DARK

We now turn to the tricks of the trade which can produce exceptions to the theoretical rules. By using the «wet watercolour» method described above it is to some extent possible to «paint» light colours over dark. For example, a white area can be «revealed» in this range of blue hills — a greyish blue, violet and dark — to which we have referred in the previous paragraph and from such a white area a few whitewashed houses can be depicted on the horizon of the foreground (Fig. 68). It is also possible to eliminate part of the green of the fields and change it to a lighter earth colour.

Producing white areas with the brush: soaking up the water and colour with the brush.

The method is simple if you remember the technique for producing white areas as explained earlier in the section on monochromes and it is all the more easy in this case where the dampness of the paper and colour can be assumed to be constant. As before, you need only clean the brush, wipe it and soak up the wash and colour on the area in question.

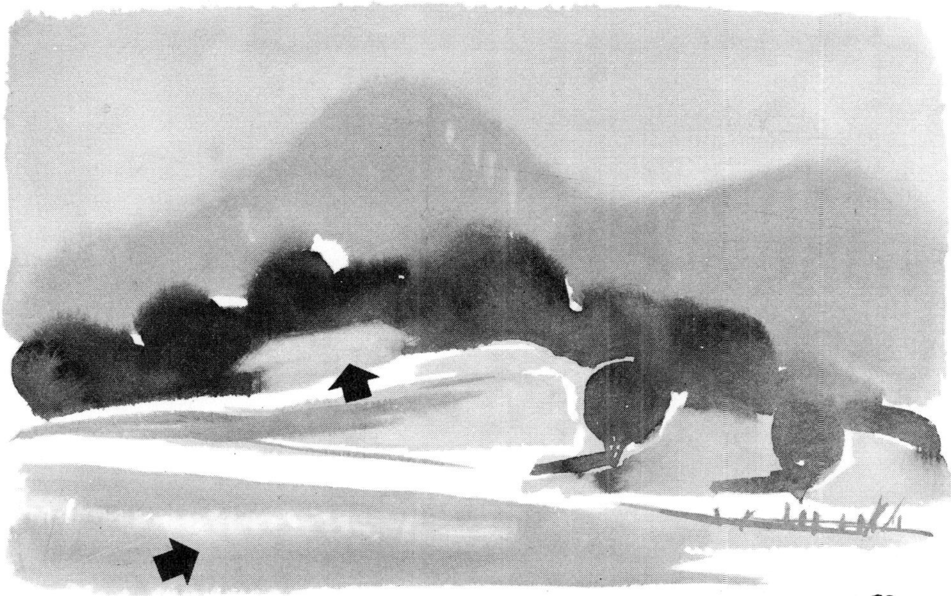

68

One clarification: this method is valid for obtaining «atmospheric whites», i.e. dirty-white areas which retain the hue of the previous colour... but this is all right in this case since pure white does not exist or at least is required for an object some distance away from the spectator. As we have said, it is also useful for changing a colour but allowance must be made for the fact that the second colour is bound to be influenced by the first. However much we try to hide the fact, the lighter earth colour mentioned earlier will have a touch of green or lemon yellow. So, remembering the rules of colour harmonization which state that the picture should consist of a specific range of colour, a dominant tone, this very slight greenish tone may well harmonize perfectly with the green of the trees. We can say then that the technique is valid.

LARGE AND SMALL WHITE AREAS... WHICH HAVE NOT BEEN MARKED OUT IN ADVANCE

The theory — and in this case practice too — says that in watercolours the white areas must be marked out in advance and produced by the white paper. Any other way would, in principle, be a trick which is unacceptable in pure watercolours. If we overlooked this rule, we should be simply making a pastiche, an undisciplined technique used by a beginner who is incapable of producing a good watercolour.

Methods for producing white areas.

So, theory — and, as I have said, practice too in this case — makes the rules and skill breaks them. Sometimes, skilled professional artists throw this rule overboard but take great care to hide the fact. In some cases it is helpful to paint with white wax and in others, with the tip of a piece of wood or the handle of the brush; or even, in extremes, to paint with white watercolour.

MAKING WHITE AREAS WITH WAX OR WAX COLOUR

If you mark a piece of white paper with a strip of pure wax, you will see that when you paint over it with diluted watercolour, the colour will not take in the waxed area so that it remains white while the surrounding areas become coloured. Therefore, for example, in order to mark out the mast of a boat and the reflection of that mast in the still water in a harbour, you need only «paint» the mast and the highlights in the water with wax (having first sketched them in with a lead pencil) and then you can paint over them with a brush soaked in colour; the waxed areas will remain a clear, pure white.

Marking out with wax

This method is sometimes used to obtain special textures of effects; not simply to mark out small white areas but for waxing larger patches with different sized strokes of wax which then produce stippled coloured planes, «rubbed» colours, irregular speckled areas, etc.

MAKING SMALL WHITE STROKES WITH THE TIP OF THE BRUSH-HANDLE

A landscape, seascape or still-life frequently contains small highlights or light areas in the shape of rather heavy regular or irregular strokes: the highlight on a branch or thin tree-trunk, the luminous profile of a small cylinder or a rather shallow plane in perspective, etc. It would require considerable pressure and trouble to mark out such a form properly in advance, allowing the white paper to show through. The common method is, therefore, to reveal or «open up» this white area with the tip of the brush-handle. For this, the tip of the handle must be cut in the shape of a wedge and the area to be «opened up» must be wet. But be careful: the wedge-shaped tip must not be sharp, newly-cut and pointed, but smooth, worn and rounded so that it produces a broad stroke in one movement without scratching or damaging the surface of the paper. Moreover, the area must only be very slightly wet and the colour only just applied but, since the area is dark and the watercolour will be only slightly diluted, it will dry very quickly. If these conditions remain, rubbing the area with some pressure using the wedge of the brush will remove the colour and easily reveal the white of the paper (Fig. 69).

«Drawing» white areas with the wedge-shaped end of the brush-handle.

...OR WITH THE NAIL OF THE THIRD OR LITTLE FINGER

Fresquet makes these lines by «drawing» with the tip of a fingernail in one quick stroke from right to left, removing the colour (Fig. 70).

... or with a fingernail.

BOLDLY PAINTING SMALL WHITE AREAS WITH WHITE WATERCOLOURS

We have already mentioned this last way in which practice prevails over theory. We have said that to obtain small white areas, dots or very

69

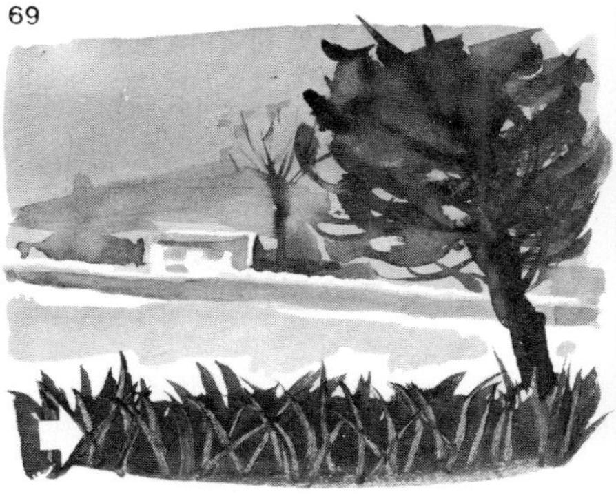

70

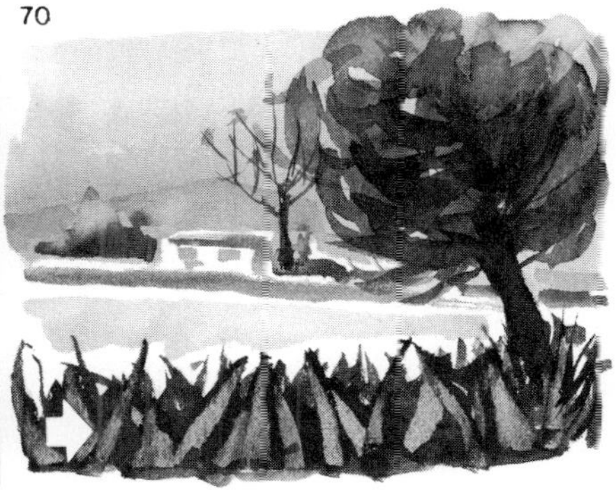

thin lines, the professional artist sometimes uses white watercolour applied rather thickly to cover the underlying colour.

Don't misapply these tricks!

So, now you know these tricks but, please, don't misapply them. Remember that a professional artist uses them but does not depend upon them. He knows that they are not superior to the normal methods and he is concerned solely with developing the medium as such, because he is well aware that watercolour does not allow trickery or legerdemain. If a watercolour is going badly and is not coming out clear and transparent, nothing can save it. It is better to put it away as reminder of what not to do.

★

When discussing monochromes, we said that watercolour is in every way similar to them. Since we have already given practical instructions in that chapter, we won't repeat ourselves by explaining again how to paint an even, flat surface, how to remove colour from an area just painted, what is a «break» and how to avoid it, how to paint a shaded area, etc. Since this knowledge can be equally applied to watercolour, we can now study this medium in practice, painting the following subjects:

PRACTICE IN PAINTING IN WATERCOLOURS

Guillermo Fresquet is here with us.

... ...

«We can begin when you're ready, Parramon.»

«Good. What do you think we should do first?»

«Let's see: I think first of all it is worth learning how to make up all the tones and colours, working only with the three primaries.»

«And black?»

«Of course; but only sometimes.»

«Right, then, while you are painting, I'll follow you, take notes and explain step by step everything you are doing. OK?»

«Fine.»

... ...

That is our plan. Fresquet will paint in watercolours while I explain what he is doing and how he is doing it, now and then pointing out any special feature. You will follow these explanations in practice, by painting, employing the same methods and following every word of Fresquet's instructions.

WITH ONLY THREE COLOURS... AND BLACK

At first Fresquet will work only with three colours, the three primaries, and black. In his watercolour box the three primaries are:

Ultramarine blue (or Prussian blue if your box contains that colour).
Carmine.
Lemon yellow (or medium cadmium yellow).

To make these instructions more effective, Fresquet and I considered it necessary to begin these practical exercises with only these three colours (and black) in view of the fact that every colour in nature can be obtained from them. You must learn and remember that:

Every colour in nature always contains a certain amount of blue, carmine and yellow.

With only three colours

Ochre is produced from a large amount of yellow, a smaller amount of carmine and an even smaller amount of blue. Olive green is composed of yellow and a rather smaller amount of blue together with a very tiny amount of carmine. Black (or rather a very dark grey) is obtained by mixing more or less equal amounts of these three colours, and so on. Once you know the potential of these three, the problem of mixing colours is solved.

While we have been discussing this, Fresquet has fixed the paper to a wooden board with a few drawing-pins to prevent it from wrinkling and cockling with the moisture. He has fetched some clean water and opened his paint-box...

Are you ready yet?

As Fresquet and I decided, we shall begin this series of practical exercises on painting in watercolours with a very specific exercise in mixing and compounding colours.

On pages 60 and 61 you can see the model to be used in this exercise. It consists of a sheet with 35 colours all obtained from the three primary colours and black.

As you will realise, this exercise is simply for practice, so that before you begin to paint a proper subject you will know what to do and what colours to mix in order to obtain any specific tone or colour. This is just an introductory step but Fresquet and I consider it absolutely essential. What's more, the success you obtain in this first exercise will most certainly have a great influence on the results of all the others.

So, keeping this in mind, we can begin.

Start by taking a sheet of watercolour paper, one of the brands mentioned earlier. Using a rather hard pencil *very faintly* draw the squares which you will use for composing the colours in the model.

Prepare the items required for this exercise: a drawing-board, paper, water, brushes, a piece of rag for drying the brushes, a scrap of paper for use as a «palette» or a surface for testing the colours, etc.

Remember that when it is moistened, real watercolour paper cockles easily, producing wrinkles which make your work more difficult. To prevent this you should use the method for mounting and stretching the paper as explained on page 17 in the section on monochromes. However, we do not think you will need to do this if you take the following precautions:

First: moisten the paper with clean water

I. Moisten the whole surface of the paper with clean water, using a wide brush, small sponge or otherwise a clean rag (if you use a rag rub very gently with the damp cloth so as not to damage the surface of the paper).

II. Place the paper on the drawing-board and leave it there for a short while to allow the surface to expand, i.e. to allow the fibre to stretch under the influence of the moisture.

Fix it to the drawing-board while still wet with drawing-pins.

III. Then, before the paper can dry, fix it to the board with eight or more drawing-pins, causing it to stretch (but not over-stretch) as it dries. If you take these precautions, there will be very few wrinkles or cockles when you come to paint.

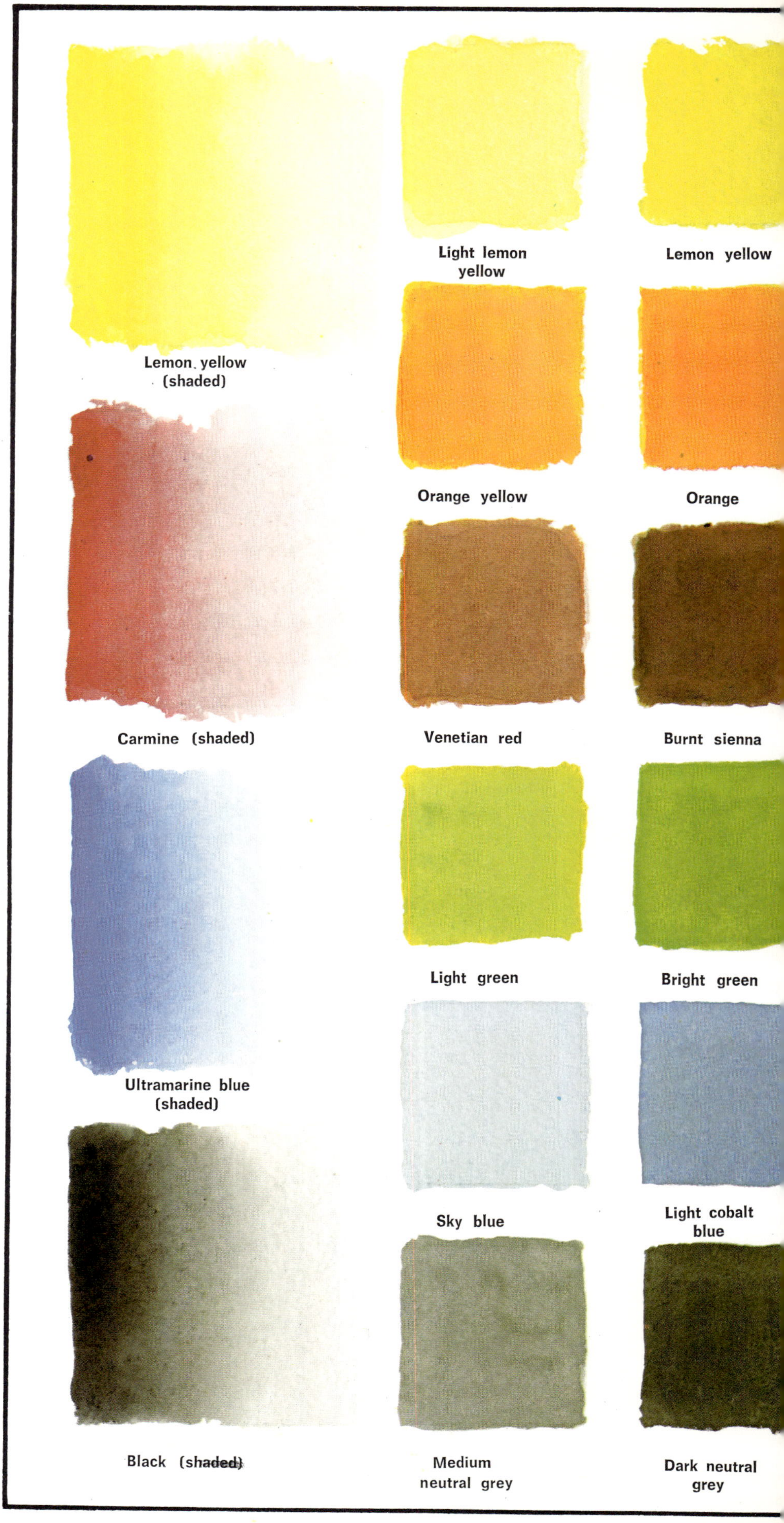
Lemon yellow (shaded)
Light lemon yellow
Lemon yellow
Orange yellow
Orange
Carmine (shaded)
Venetian red
Burnt sienna
Light green
Bright green
Ultramarine blue (shaded)
Sky blue
Light cobalt blue
Black (shaded)
Medium neutral grey
Dark neutral grey

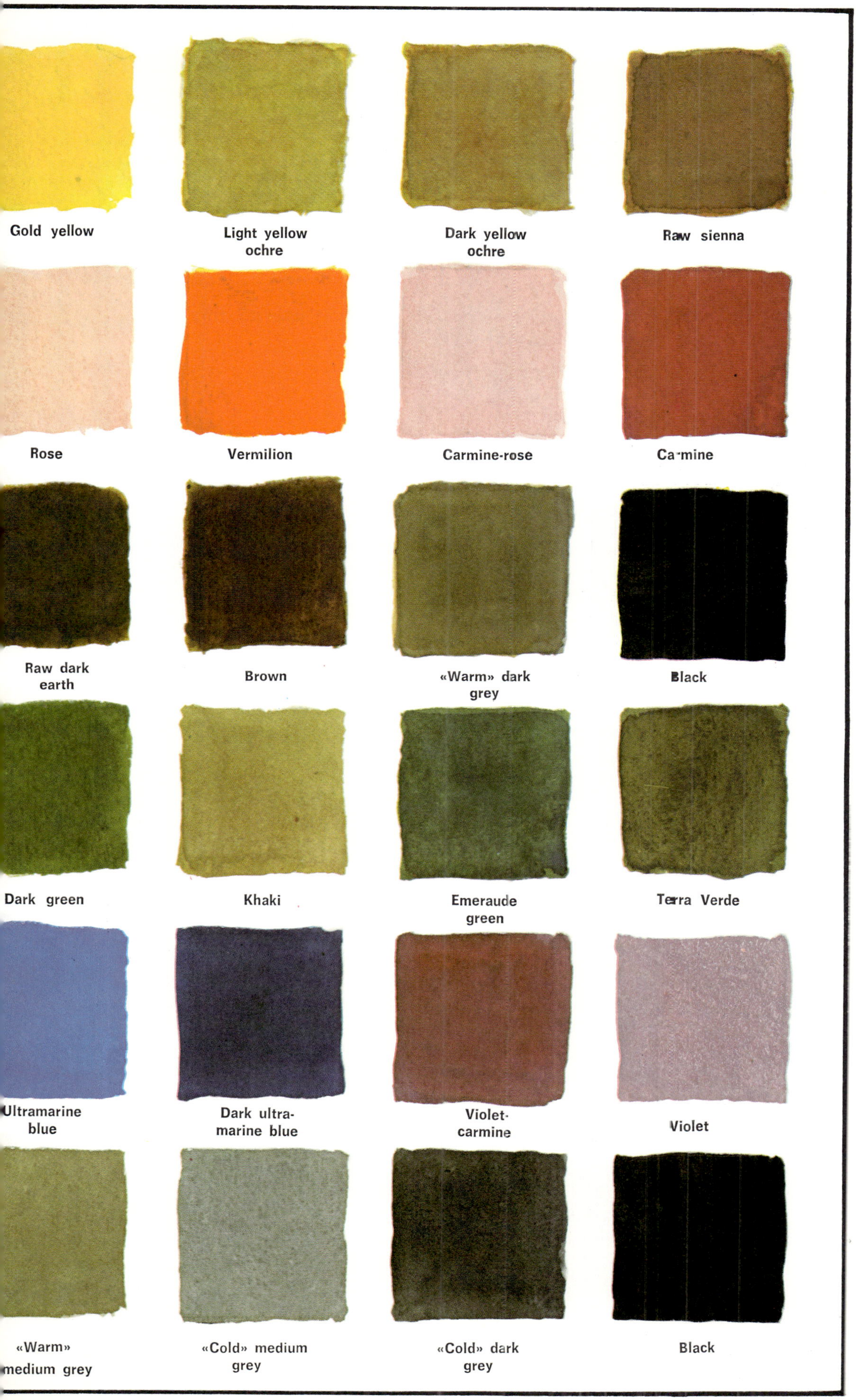
Gold yellow
Light yellow ochre
Dark yellow ochre
Raw sienna
Rose
Vermilion
Carmine-rose
Carmine
Raw dark earth
Brown
«Warm» dark grey
Black
Dark green
Khaki
Emeraude green
Terra Verde
Ultramarine blue
Dark ultra-marine blue
Violet-carmine
Violet
«Warm» medium grey
«Cold» medium grey
«Cold» dark grey
Black

When carrying out these first exercises, I suggest that you remove the unnecessary colours from your box to prevent any confusion.

Hold the scrap of paper you are going to use for testing the colours. Use a No. 10 brush.

And now, before you begin, let me remind you that:

The colours — the primaries — which you must use for this and the next two exercises are:

Lemon yellow
Carmine
Ultramarine blue
(and black)

THE EXERCISE

Using the method already learnt, begin by painting simple shaded areas with the lemon yellow, carmine, ultramarine blue and black without mixing them: These are shown down the left of the example. (See pages 60 and 61).

Now paint specimen colours, working from left to right. To obtain the right colour in each case you must:

1. Read the description of each colour, in accordance with the following instructions.
2. Mix the colour in the proper hollows of the paint-box.
3. Test the shade obtained on the «palette».
4. Paint the final colour.

Obviously it would be preferable for you to obtain the right colour at your first attempt without having to add further coats or without having to «soak up» the colour, that is to lower it by removing some of it. However, you will usually have to change some colours. When doing so, remember these two rules:

It is always better to «throw in the towel».

a) If you make a mistake, it is always better to «throw in the towel» and then strengthen or change it by means of another coat.

b) In principle, it is best to change the colour by working on a wet area. However, a final coat will be needed and this must be put on when the previous one is dry.

THESE ARE THE COLOURS IN THE ORDER THEY ARE TO BE PAINTED

Light lemon yellow .... Simply with lemon yellow and water.

Lemon yellow .... The yellow pastille, slightly thick to make it strong.

Gold yellow .... First strong yellow as before. Then, while the yellow is drying, add a very light wash of carmine (Careful! carmine is very strong. A mere touch of it is enough to produce a rose colour as required here).

Light yellow ochre .... First obtain a gold yellow as above. Add a small amount of blue and black while the first coat is still wet.
(Be careful with the blue and black! They are strong. If you don't take care the result will be too strong).

Dark yellow ochre .... As above, adding a very small amount of carmine, blue and black.

Raw sienna .... Begin by mixing gold yellow. Leave it for a few moments to acquire body and really tint the paper. Take care: before it is completely dry, add a carmine-violet which is obtained from carmine and a little blue with just enough water. It is important for this violet wash to have a slight touch of carmine.

Orange yellow .... Very thick paste-like yellow with carmine added when still wet. Gradually increase the amount of carmine until you obtain the colour in the model.

Orange .... As above with more carmine.

Rose .... Carmine diluted with water and a touch of yellow.

Vermilion .... A lot of yellow, thick and paste-like, then add carmine which must not be too strong so that the yellow can «breathe».

Carmine-rose .... Carmine diluted with a large amount of water and a touch of blue.

Carmine .... First a wash of blue. Then, while the blue wash is still slightly wet, add strong carmine.

Venetian red .... First mix a rather bright orange and then, while it is wet, add a little blue to make it greyer. This should produce a sienna with carmine as the dominant tone.

Burnt sienna .... Strong, paste-like yellow and carmine to produce a rather bright orange. Then while wet, add some blue and a large amount of black. It may be necessary to add more carmine to obtain this dark reddish colour.

Raw dark earth .... We are now dealing with rather dark colours which are therefore capable of covering. In such cases you must of course work with thicker, heavier colours and less water. The right way to obtain this colour in successive stages is firstly to produce a dark ochre by using a lot of yellow, a little carmine and a little blue. Then mix a raw sienna (still using only a little water and painting while wet, mixing on the actual paper, as it were). Finally, make the colour stronger with the three primaries, darkening the sienna and adding black if necessary. This should produce a dark earth colour with a cold tint, i.e. rather bluish.

«Warm» dark grey .... It is important to obtain this «warmth» which is produced by a dark yellow ochre in the dominant grey. To make this colour you must in principle mix the three primaries in more or less equal amounts, applying them onto a dry coat of dark yellow ochre. In practice, however, you can make use of black and white which will give grey.
All you need add is a little ochre (made up from gold yellow and a little blue and black). Either way, it is not a difficult colour to obtain. (As you know, grey is always lying in wait in your palette, ready to pounce). One warning: do not use the white as a covering, paste-like colour but dilute it with water so that it acts as a colour while becoming transparent).

Black .... The black pastille, slightly thick so that it covers.

Light green .... A rather bright yellow and a little blue.

Bright green .... As above but with more blue.

Dark green .... As above, with more blue and a little black.

Khaki .... Begin by mixing a light green. Then while it is wet, paint on a little carmine and yellow. It may be necessary to add more blue and yellow and possibly a touch of black.

Viridian............................ As you know, viridian green is a strong bluish green. So you will obtain it from yellow and a lot of blue, nothing else.

Terra Verde	Strong paste-like yellow and a very small amount of blue which will produce a dirty olive green. While wet, quickly add a little blue.
Sky blue	Well diluted blue and, while wet, a touch of yellow to offset the purple tinge of the ultramarine blue. Use only a very small amount of yellow, so that it does not change the bluish shade.
Cobalt blue	Strong blue but not paste-like (we could call it slightly stronger than medium blue), adding a little yellow as before to offset the purple tinge of the ultramarine blue.
Ultramarine blue	Only blue, thick but not paste-like.
Dark ultramarine blue	Thick, paste-like blue with a little carmine and black (very little of these two).
Violet-carmine	Blue and carmine, the latter being stronger, letting through the white of the paper, that is to say, diluted with enough water.
Violet	A wash of blue and carmine, more transparent than above, that is, with more water.
Medium neutral grey	Watercolour white and black, both diluted enough to be transparent, allowing the white paper to have an effect.
Dark neutral grey	As above with more black.
«Warm» medium grey	Watercolour white and black, producing a medium grey. Add a little yellow and carmine in keeping with the «warm» tinge.
«Cold» medium grey	First mix a neutral grey as before. Then add a little blue while still wet.
«Cold» dark grey	As before, increasing the black and blue.
Black	The black pastille, thick enough to cover.

A SPECIFIC EXERCISE USING THREE COLOURS ONLY

FRESQUET PAINTS AN APPLE

Fresquet begins by quickly sketching the apple with a No. 2 crayon, producing a two-dimensional unshaded drawing (Fig. 19).

Then, using a thick brush, rather casually he wests the surface of the drawing with clean water, simply trying to moisten it.

«With only a little water, very little. You see?», Fresquet remarks. «As you know, the aim of this first wash is to remove any gum left on the paper so that the washes are more liquid».

First stage: moisten the paper with clean water.

You understand? Before beginning to paint, it is always advisable to moisten the paper — with a very little water — to remove any remains of grease or gum which may have come from your hand while you were drawing or which may have been left on the paper.

Fresquet now waits until the surface is dry and...

FIRST STAGE (FIG. 20)

...begins to paint.

He paints the entire apple — leaving out the white area of the highlight — with a coat of lemon yellow, the ordinary intensity, diluted but retaining enough colour.

Here — and always — Fresquet seems to paint in a rather off-hand manner and astonishingly quickly without being too fussy... but keeping within the outline of the model which is — I repeat — not firm and absolute.

While the yellow is still fresh and wet — completely wet — Fresquet now adds a few strokes of carmine weakened with water. He does no more than stipple it, painting patches which may seem confused but which are in fact situated in the dark sections of the apple. But look... the wetness of the yellow and carmine causes the carmine to spread and blend so that the initial patches automatically disappear and the two colours combine to produce an orange colour.

«Wet» painting.

SECOND STAGE (FIG. 21)

Still painting while the surface is wet, Fresquet heightens the yellow, cleans his brush and adds carmine as before in irregular patches which are mixed and blend with the yellow due to the moisture.

Fig. 19. — Fresquet does not make a careful drawing as a basis of the subject to be painted. Here he only makes a few strokes to outline the apple.

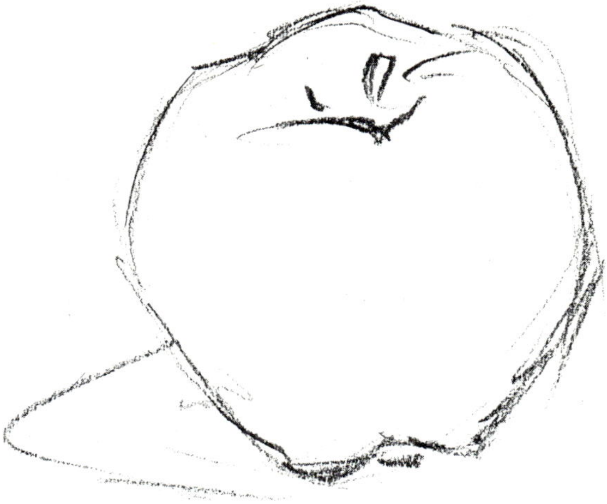

Fig. 20. — Notice here the effect obtained by superimposing carmine on yellow, painting while wet, that is to say while the yellow is wet, and then, apparently haphazardly, applying a few patches of carmine which are blended due to the moisture.

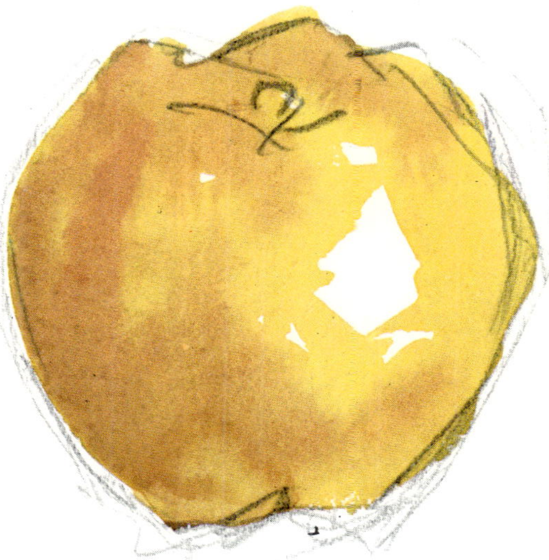

Fig. 21. — Still working on a wet surface, applying coats on previous wet coats, Fresquet produces a perfectly blended colour effect and at the same time obtains smooth, spontaneous shading. Notice how when painting in this «fresh» manner, the artist is concerned with producing the form or volume of the fruit.

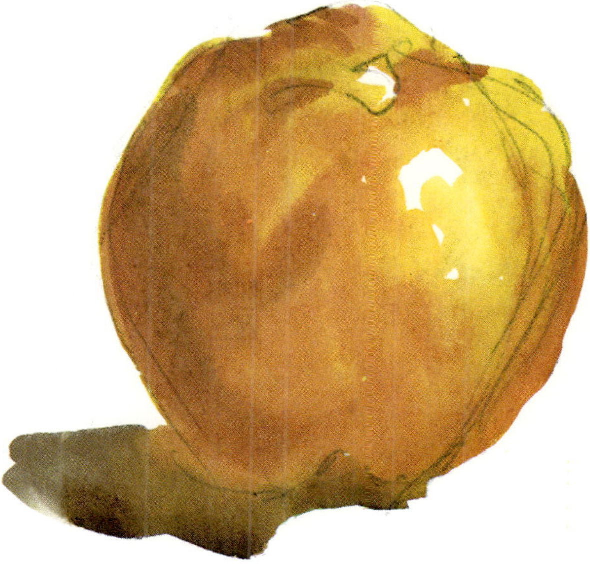

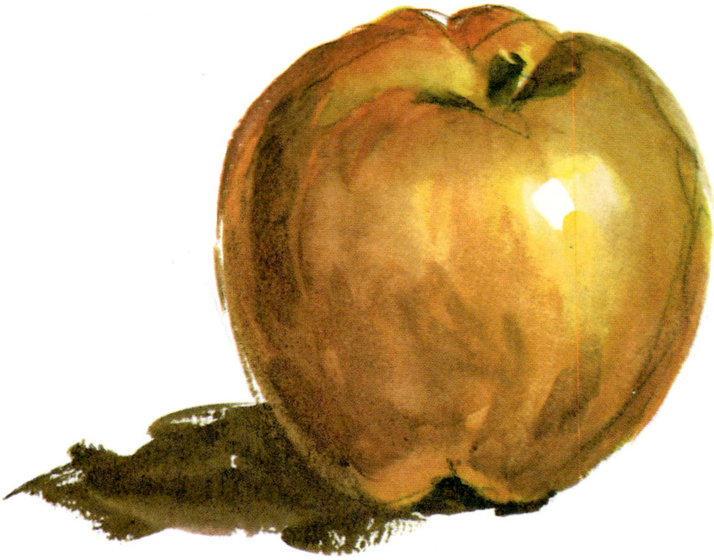

Figs. 22 and 23. — Above, Fresquet shows us an advanced stage of this exercise, having obtained the full form with only the colouring and final details lacking.
Below, the finished work, after applying the techniques of soaking up water and colour, using the brush as a sponge in order to change and adjust colours.

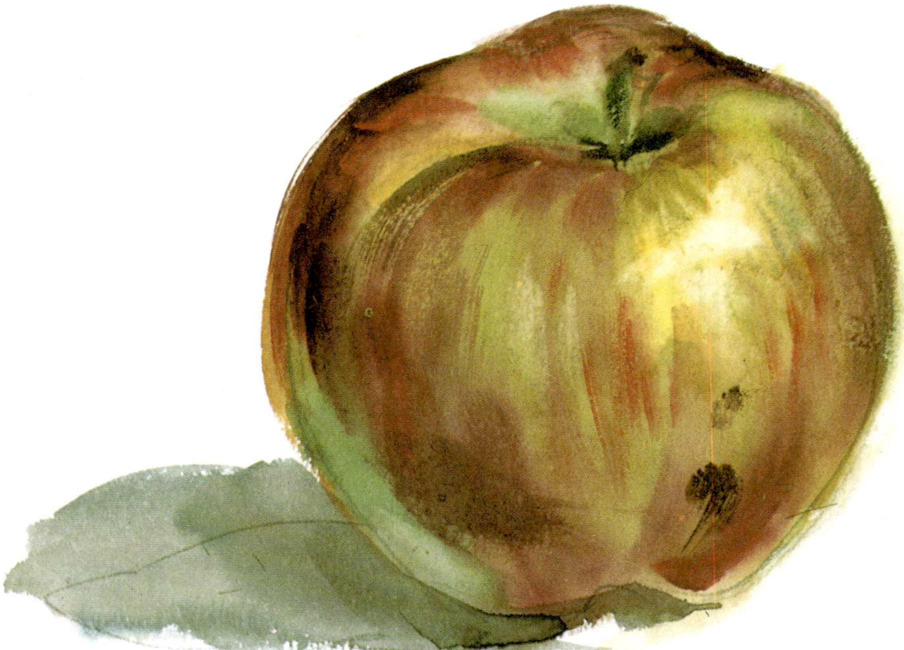

Now he mixes yellow, carmine and a little blue, producing an earth colour with a carmine tinge. He tests these colours on the scrap of paper which he keeps beside his rag. He applies it more strongly in the shadowed areas. He dries his brush on the rag WITHOUT WASHING IT, and gently stroking those areas, blends the shading of this darker colour with the previous orange shade.

He now makes the colour of the shadow cast by the apple: a touch of yellow, a touch of carmine, more blue and a bit of black. He tests it on the scrap of paper, corrects it by reducing the carmine, and paints the shadow almost in one stroke from left to right. When this colour reaches the shape of the apple, the orange tint mingles with the grey in the shadow.

THIRD STAGE (FIG. 22)

While still wet... less so.

You must remember in fact that as the work advances following the upwards and outwards system, the colours are less diluted and thicker every time. So, of course, the moisture is reduced, producing firmer brush-strokes.

Method and mixtures.

Fresquet outlines the fruit with touches of carmine and blue mixed with a little yellow and thus produces this carmine-tinted sienna. He emphasizes the more shaded areas, adding a little black to the other three colours.

He now adds paint and soaks it up in succession, from time to time applying the clean, wiped brush, removing colour and revealing lighter areas.

He suddenly stops painting. So far he has been working feverishly. He has reached this stage in just under fifteen minutes.

He carefully studies the model and his painting... emphasizes the colour of the shadow by painting with blue and carmine, looks for a dirty grey colour in the hollows of his box, adds a touch of this dirty grey to the shadow while it is wet...

He stops again.

«It's going all right,» he remarks, «but it still has a dirty tint, rather too much carmine and orange».

FOURTH AND LAST STAGE (FIG. 23)

With a clean brush and clean water, Fresquet wets the left-hand side of the apple and the shadow. He soaks up all the colour, leaving the area a light, dirty grey with a dominant cream colour. He tints this area with a brighter grey containing a blue tinge. He emphasizes the light reflected from the apple (the bluish-green strip on the right in Fig. 23) with a little yellow, allowing the moisture to spread it...

He washes and soaks up water and colour in the centre and front of the fruit...

He adds yellow... a little blue...

He draws and paints simultaneously with the rather dirty carmine (taking from the «palette» and hollows in the box the rest of the bluish grey mixes) that sort of border which outlines the apple...

Light green near the stem...

Carmine and black in the more shadowed areas along the left-hand edge... yellow in the centre...

Working feverishly, painting on the wet surface, Fresquet produces shading, rapidly soaking up water and colour, emphasizing, reducing... giving form and colour to the model until he obtains the final result shown in Fig. 23.

Last of all, when the watercolour can be considered dry, he uses an almost dry brush (the bristles forming a swathe) to paint the cross-strokes, red patches and the dark bruise on the lower left-hand side...

«Do you think that's all right?»

«Perfect».

... ...

FRESQUET PAINTS A STILL-LIFE

Still working with only the three primary colours (and black), Fresquet is ready to paint the still-life shown on pages 74 and 75.

Arranging a new subject.

He has prepared and arranged the subject. Against a wall at the end of a table he has placed a cloth. On it he puts an apple, two bananas, a green ceramic vase and a lemon.

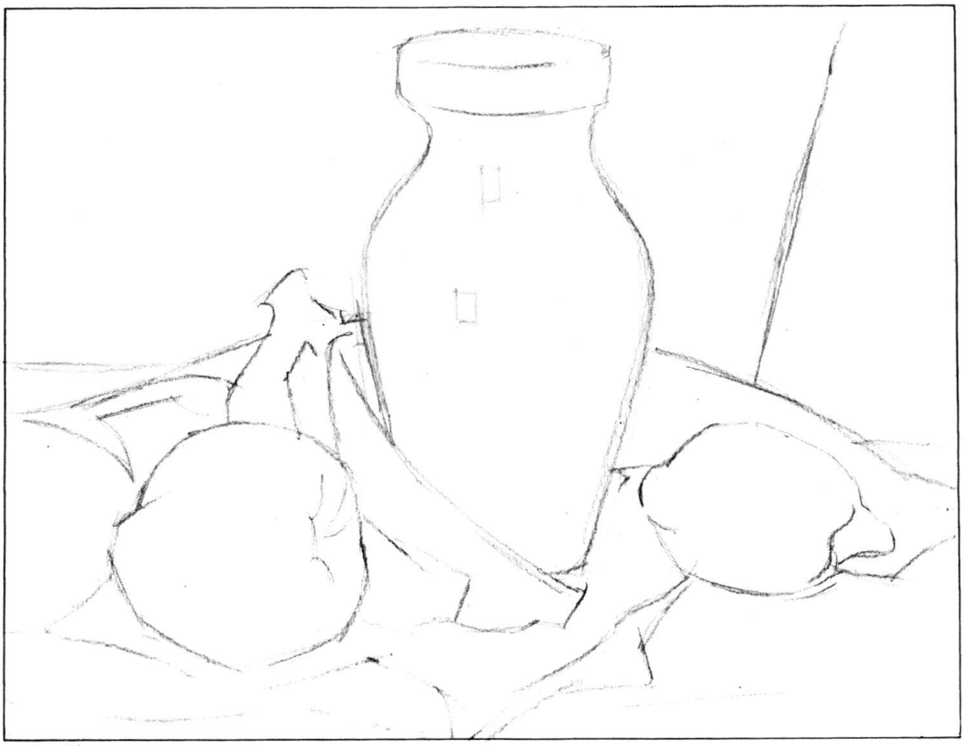

24

Like all good watercolourists, Fresquet has mastered the art of drawing. These few strokes are enough to site the model before beginning to paint.

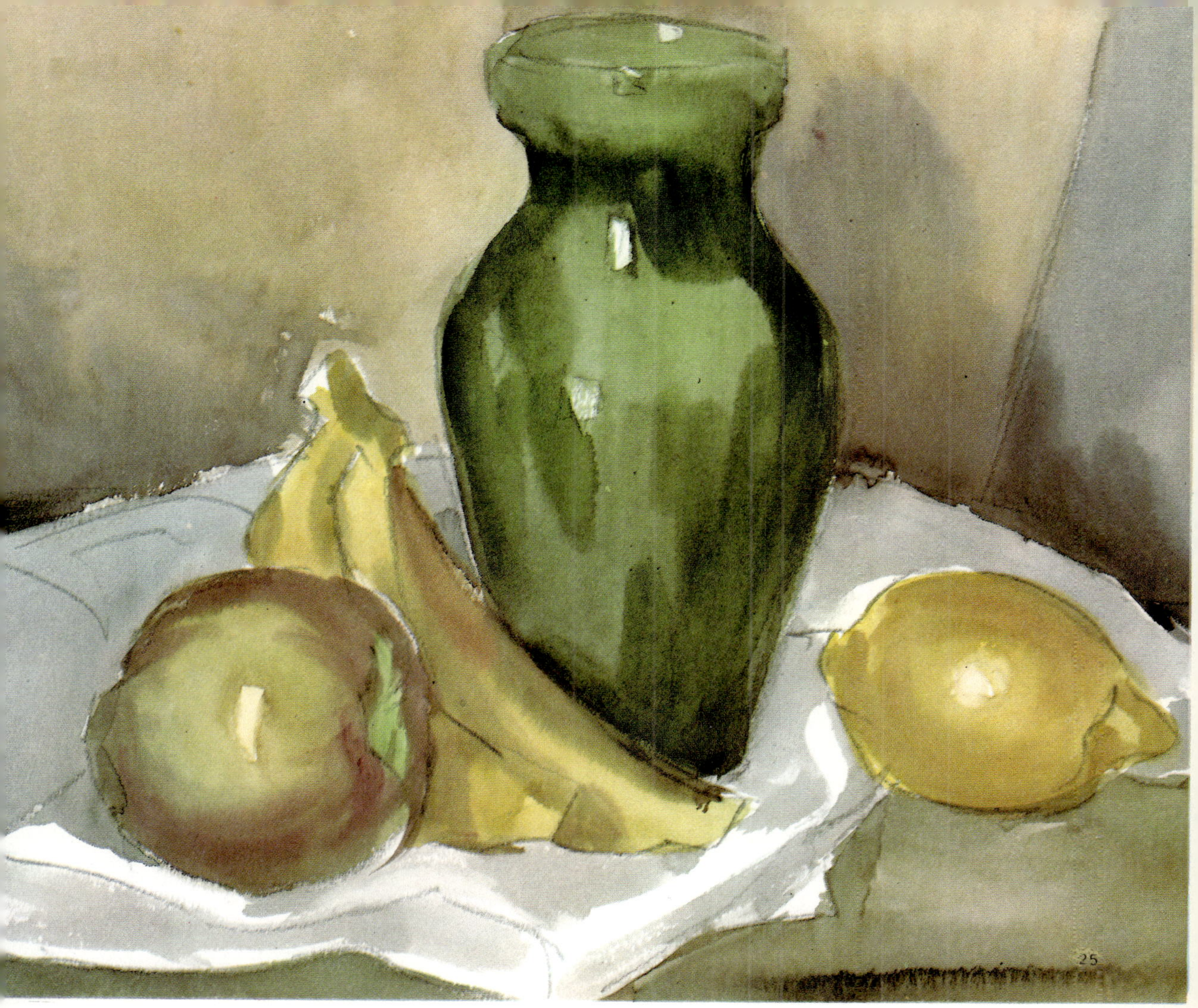

FIRST STAGE (FIG. 24)

Fresquet begins by filling in the model with rapid strokes. First he does the vase, then he outlines the bananas and apple, then the lemon... sketches in the shape of the tablecloth with a few lines, and begins to paint.

Need for perfect mastery of drawing.

(I should mention in passing, that a good watercolourist has above all to be a good drawer; able to construct the object while painting, to draw and paint simultaneously. Consequently, Fresquet does not bother to draw the details. He knows that in due course he will be able to put in the details with colour which makes his watercolour more artistic).

As before, Fresquet first wets the paper with clean water.

Without waiting for it to dry, he very rapidly adds the basic colours.

These are his colours
This is the order he follows:

Background, starting on the left: dirty ochre consisting mainly of yellow, carmine and black with a lot of water.

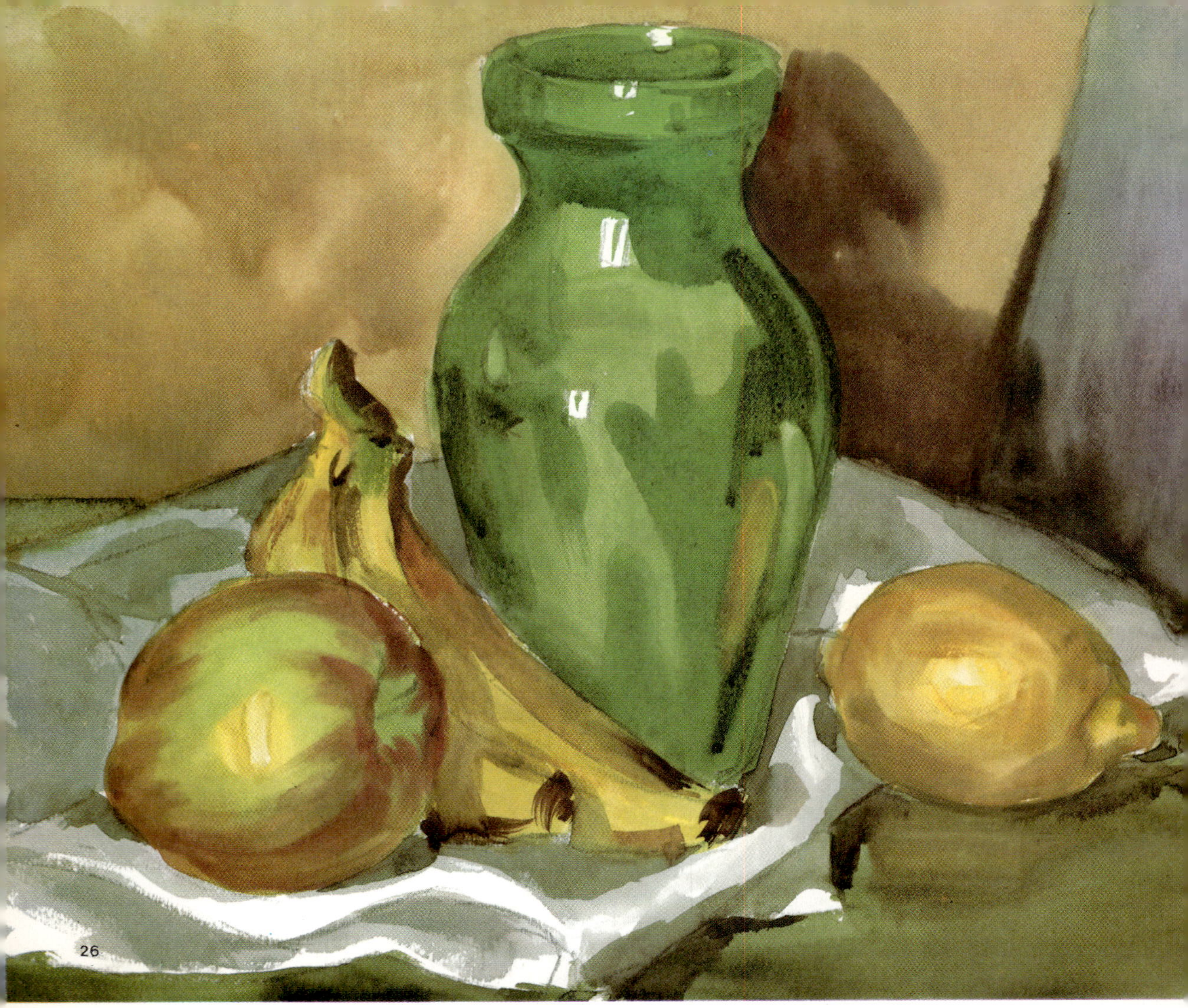

26

Right background: without washing his brush, he takes a little blue and black... a little water to weaken it... tests it on the scrap of paper... and paints. He strengthens the colour with blue and black and, while it is wet, paints in the shading which outlines the tablecloth.

Method and mixtures

Vase: a coat of light green (yellow and blue), leaving out the highlights, and, while wet, another coat with more colour, using a darker, thicker green, sketching in and beginning to give volume with the brighter strokes. A few touches of blue-black around the edges.

Tablecloth: blue-black, using the previous mixtures and those indefinable colours which are always to be found in the hollows of the box.

Apple: without cleaning his brush, he takes yellow, mixes it in the box with the previous grey and paints just with that, leaving out the highlight. Then he takes some yellow and «leaves» it on the first coat. The moisture spreads and blends it.

Lemon: he switches to the lemon and, after washing his brush, takes yellow and water. He gives it the first coat, leaving out the white area.

Bananas: an overall coat, done quickly with the same yellow.

Apple: (the previous coat is still wet). He goes back to his box in order to use the dirty grey mixtures. He takes carmine... a little blue... more carmine... water and paints the darker areas of the apple.

Table in foreground. He mixes the greenish grey with the left-over grey mixtures, a little yellow and blue. He paints with plenty of water.

Lemon. He goes over the lemon again with a yellow ochre, shaping it. Since it is not completely dry, the colour spreads and blends but Fresquet has to help in shading the luminous section in the centre. He does this by wiping the brush on the rag and soaking up the colour...

Bananas (still wet): he takes the greenish-grey mixed for the table (foreground) and gives the bananas volume with those vague greenish touches. Next he uses a brushful of orange on one of them.

SECOND STAGE (FIG. 25)

We shall not follow him in detail. The figure itself is enough to show that Fresquet has worked with a range of colours similar but stronger than those mentioned earlier.

Fresquet continues to work on wet surfaces for nearly every coat.

As before, he began with the background using a wash of light sienna, then strengthening it while wet by applying these bluish and carmine shades. He has darkened the other colours, making their tones more definite by superimposing further coats and in nearly every case working while the previous ones were still wet (almost imperceptibly wet but enough to stump the edges and blend the shading automatically) except in areas such as the sections of the tablecloth and bananas where dry, vivid strokes can be seen in firm outline. He has begun to superimpose dark greens on the vase, mixing them from blue, yellow and black. The peculiar carmine patches of the apple can already be perceived.

THIRD AND LAST STAGE (MODEL)

In the model reproduced in actual size in the next two pages, we can see the finished watercolour painted by Fresquet.

Fresquet took two hours (or, to be precise, one hour and fifty minutes) to produce this superb work. Notice and study the sections which show that he has worked on wet surfaces and also those painted dry and even with an almost dry brush, scraping the colour (look at the upper left-hand edge of the apple).

Examine carefully the colouring of the green vase which was obtained by superimposed brush-strokes, leaving out the highlights and reflected lights and adjusting the colour to that of the model, which is the only way of producing an artistic representation of reality.

Every shadow contains blue.

Remember that every shadow contains blue (sometimes with black). Do not forget that to make a colour greyer, blue is always necessary and that any dirty colour contains blue.

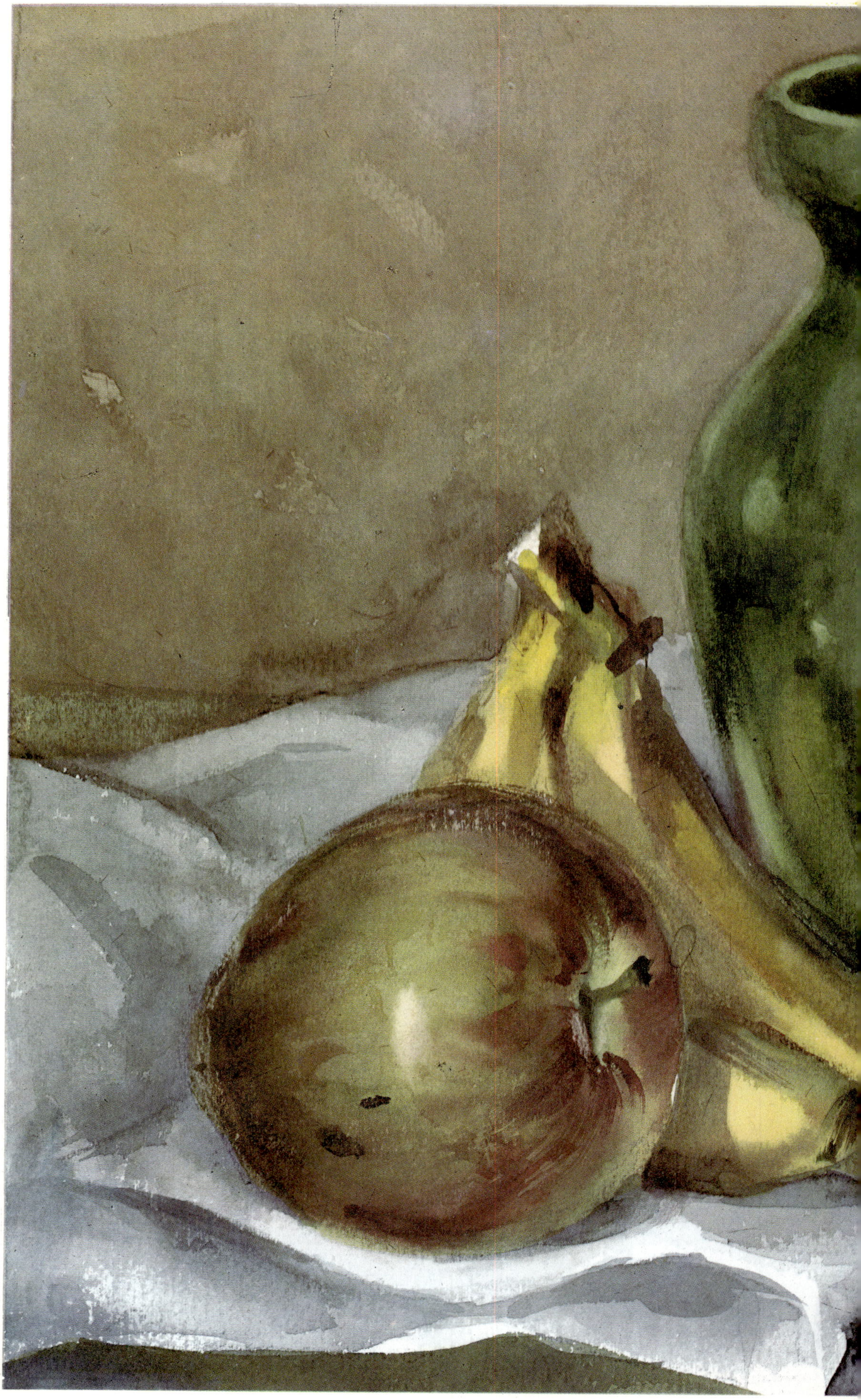

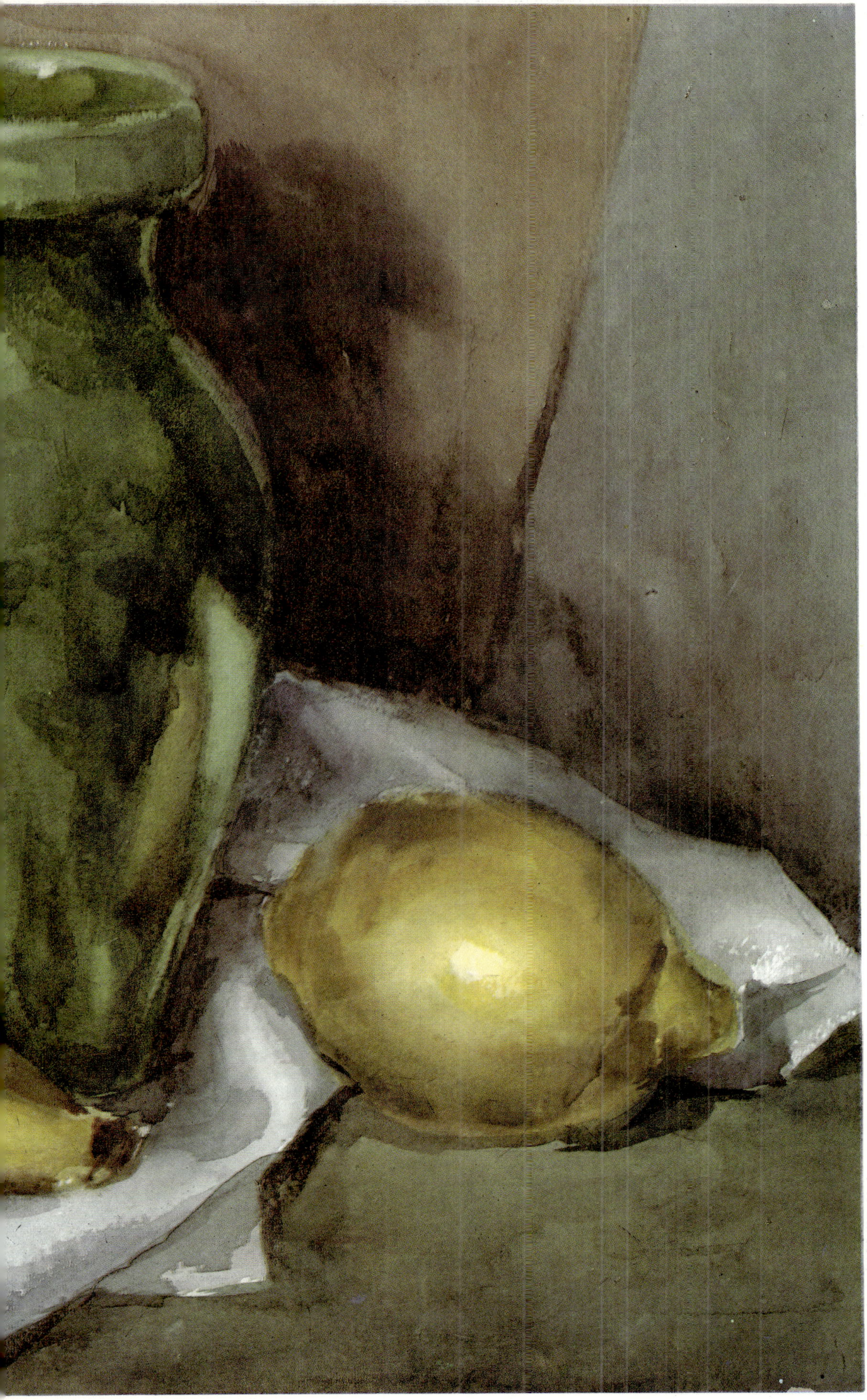

PAINTING WITH WATERCOLOUR (II)

USING EVERY COLOUR

No more restrictions! First you painted monochromes in only one colour: black. Then came watercolours but still using only three colours: blue, carmine and yellow (with black). Finally, we reach watercolours using every colour without restrictions.

The need to have practised with three colours.

You cannot calculate or multiply without having learnt how to add up. You would deceive yourself if you claimed that you could obtain colours by mixing or if you tried to produce satisfactory grey areas and perfect shading without having gained the practical experience contained in the previous instructions.

So, to sum up, the rule is:

> **Do not begin to paint with every colour in your box until you have practised and obtained every colour in nature by using only the three primaries: blue, carmine and yellow (with the help of black).**

Assuming that you have practised thoroughly with the three primaries, we shall now return to Guillermo Fresquet and paint with every colour.

«*You tell us, Fresquet*».

«*Well, we could begin with the method I use myself before painting a picture: looking for the subject, choosing it, studying its possibilities...*»

CHOICE AND PRELIMINARY STUDY OF THE SUBJECT

Factors which determine the choice of subject.

When discussing watercolours of landscapes — the most suitable subject for this medium — Fresquet tells us that he does not find a subject by chance but employs a process of analysis and search which is governed by three factors: (a) memory and experience of earlier images; (b) knowledge of locations which are rich with artistic scenes and (c) the selective ability based in the last analysis upon skill in composition.

Owing to his memory and experience of the pictures he has painted previously — some satisfactory, others not — the professional artist is undoubtedly in a better position to discriminate and choose when confronted with a new subject. It is equally true to say that «locations rich in artistic scenes» do exist and are known to the artist and one could claim, for example, that merely the sight of a leafy spot with trees bordering a river in a rather hilly terrain is enough to make the artist realise immediately that here is a subject for a picture. His capacity for immediate selection will then come into play, drawing upon his knowledge and experience of composition.

To enable the amateur to remedy this natural lack of experience, Fresquet gives the following advice:

Advice to amateurs on choosing and making the preliminary study of a subject

1) STUDY AND GAIN EXPERIENCE FROM OTHERS BY ANALYSING WORKS BY THE MASTERS.

Visit exhibitions or, if impossible, study good reproductions, cutting out and filing pictures from periodicals and journals which contain paintings by recognized artists: try to build up a small but select library of art-books. Then analyse these reproductions by studying them and even drawing small sketches of them so that you are forming and developing your selective ability. To sum up, «crib» the experience of recognized artists until your taste is formed and you are capable of selecting subjects for yourself.

Visit exhibitions; study good reproductions.

2) VISIT LOCATIONS FREQUENTED BY ARTISTS.

That means going to places which have already been painted and where artists are known to paint. This is not just theoretical advice. You know, in fact, that such-and-such a town is frequented by painters, that such-and-such a district of the city is sometimes visited by professionals or expert amateurs with easel set up and palette in hand, that painters go to a particular part of the harbour, that the landscapes in such-and-such a region are or have been taken as the subject of paintings, etc. This method of «painting where others paint» gradually forms the ability to be one oneself, to discover new places and paint original subjects.

Characteristic locations.

3) STUDY COMPOSITION AND PRACTISE IT BEFOREHAND BY DRAWING SMALL SKETCHES BEFORE PAINTING THE FINAL PICTURE.

When the time comes to decide upon the most suitable framework, viewpoint, light, contrast, etc. — besides remembering and taking into

Preliminary study by making two or three sketches.

consideration the compositional schemes studied in reproductions of famous paintings — it will be best to make two or three preliminary sketches. Not only amateurs but most professionals do this, including Fresquet and myself.

GENERAL RULES FOR COMPOSING A LANDSCAPE

It is, however, necessary to remember some of the traditional rules for obtaining a good landscape composition while also remembering that the art of composition is not the result of rules and logic but is something inherent (not that it cannot be cultivated and developed).

General analysis

Above all, you must exhaust every possibility. By that I mean examine the subject from every possible angle, analysing the location of some shapes in relation to others and trying to obtain contrasts in colour and shapes. The direction, intensity and quality of the light are important in this connection. Also take into account the frame which can be envisaged by using an ordinary black cardboard frame enclosing an area of some four to six inches (Fig. 1).

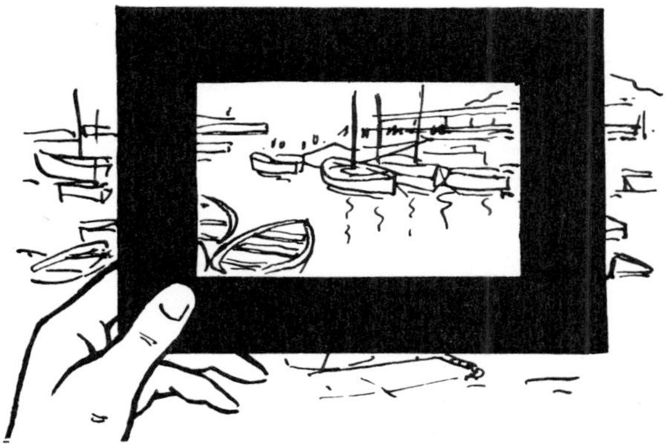

Fig. 1. — The model cannot move but you can. Study every possible angle. Look at it from above, below, and sideways. To envisage the frame, use a cardboard frame as illustrated here.

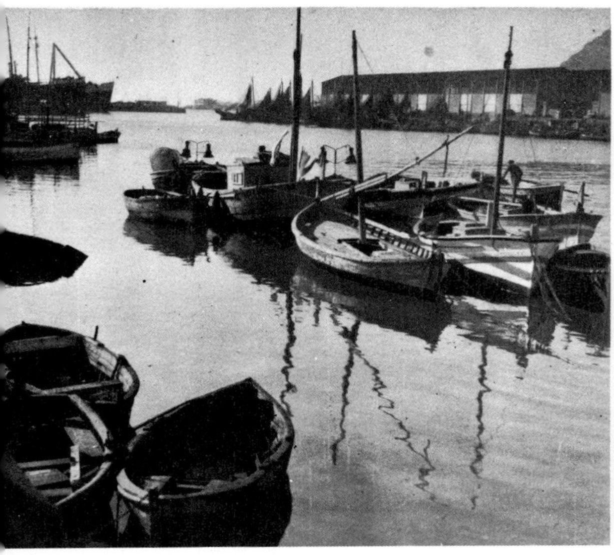

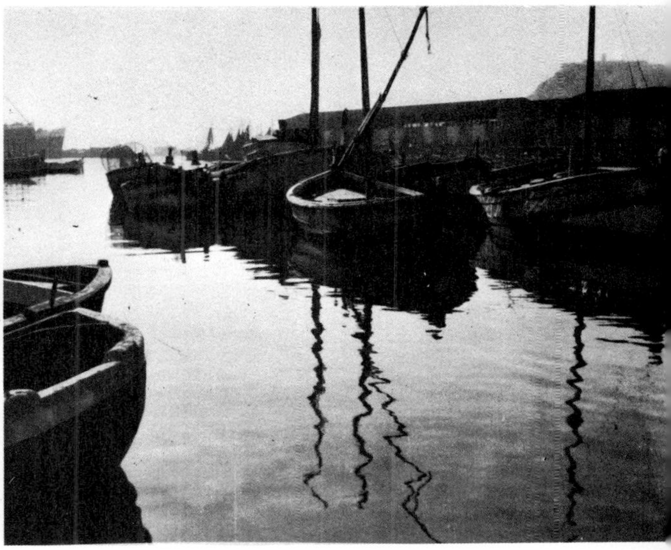

It is worth remembering — and applying in the early stages — the traditional composition of a landscape based upon a subject providing a prominent foreground backed by two or more planes which increase the sense of depth. Then bear in mind that this foreground is emphasized and brought out both by shapes and tonal contrasts. This traditional formula can be discarded later when you have enough experience and knowledge to choose more original and freer compositions (Fig. 2).

Traditional formula: foreground prominent.

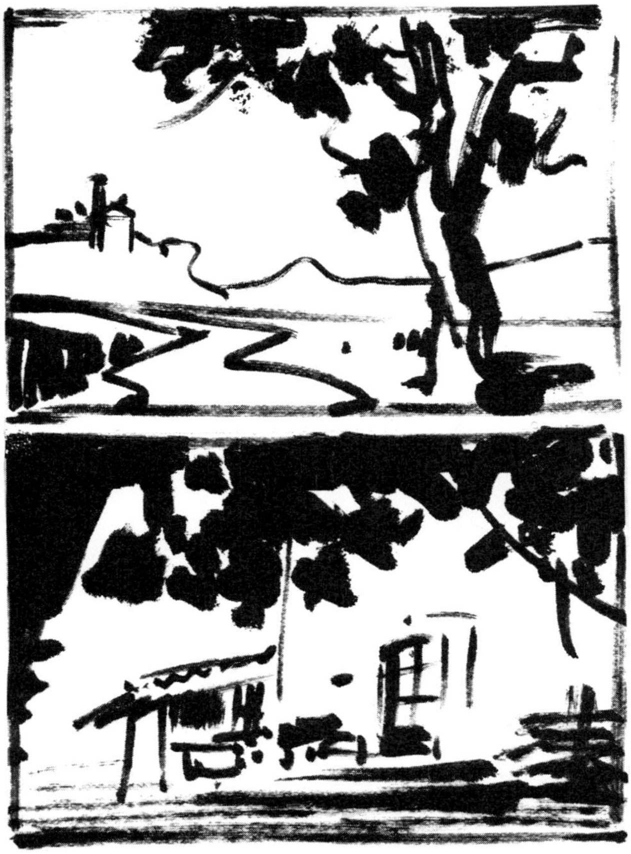

Fig. 2. — The formula of framing the image with a foreground prominent in shape and tone, produces safe results in composition.

Notice that this foreground also acts as a perspective plane which produces the sense of depth while also increasing the necessary unity of composition.

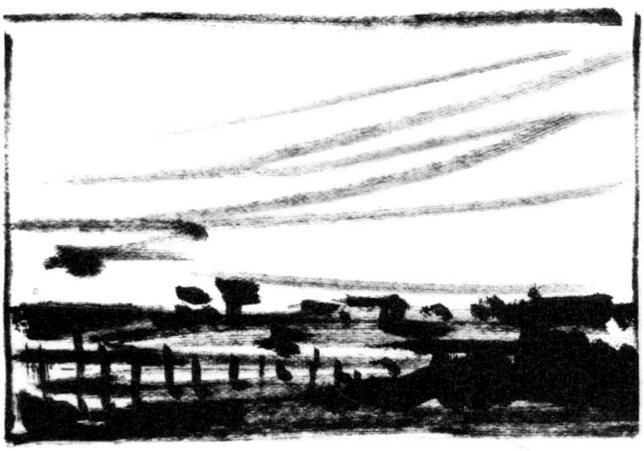

Fig. 3. — Large skies with low horizons are always an effective subject.

Do not place the horizon in the centre.

The tonal and chromatic mass of the sky can in many cases be a decisive factor when arranging and harmonizing the composition. This can be verified in watercolours especially where cloudy skies can produce decorative effects and also be the occasion for great technical brilliance. We are thinking here of extensive skies occupying three-quarters of the picture. For composition purpose, it will never be advisable to place the horizon in the centre of the picture (Fig. 3).

Perspective as a factor.

Finally, when composing landscapes, do not overlook the possibility of using perspective as a factor which creates unity within the framework of variety, remembering that to produce this you should place yourself where the perspective — the meeting point of lines running towards the horizon — is not too obvious (Fig. 4).

What is left?
Of course, the light.

Do not paint in a noon light.

Unless you decide to paint a landscape with a cloudy sky (which I do not recommend. since what you are looking for in the early stages is a model with clearcut lights and shadows, evident volume and well-stressed contrast), I advise you to paint before or after midday, thus avoiding the period when the sunlight is vertical and more or less eliminates shadows from objects or makes them unpleasant.

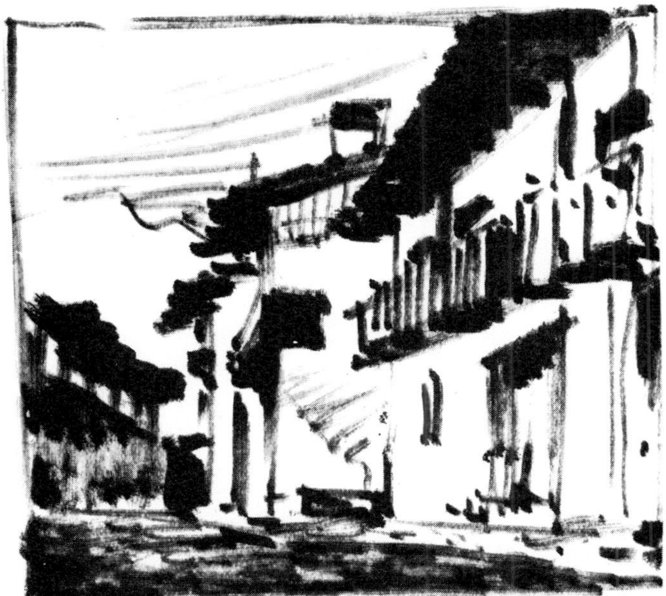

Fig. 4. — Remember the possibility of using perspective effects as a means of imposing order on the composition. But do not make these effects obvious, avoiding a well-ordered, monotonous arrangement.

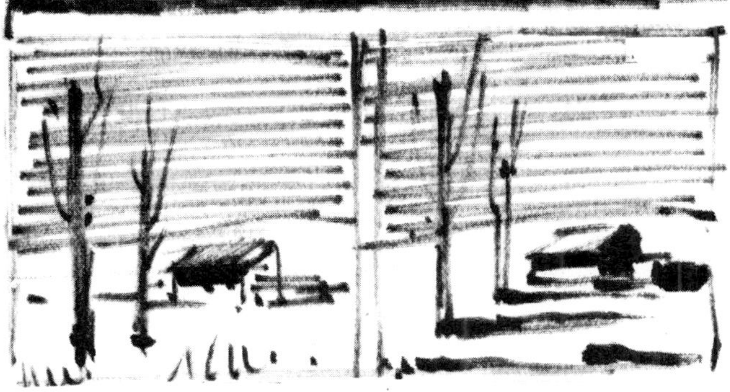

Fig. 5. — Do not paint at noon when the sun is at its height. Shadow either does not exist or is unpleasant.

FRESQUET EXAMINES THE COMPOSITION OF A PICTURE

A professional such as Guillermo Fresquet may well realise straight away that a subject or object in front of him is worth putting on canvas (or paper in this case), if the light is at its best — «here and now» — for emphasizing the values of the model, or that the shape, arrangement, colour and contrast between the various planes can together produce a good picture. But, as Fresquet himself admits, the professional usually wants to confirm this first impression, grasping it and perfecting it by means of a simple pencil drawing.

Sometimes Fresquet begins by studying the composition with a couple of sketches.

You can see in Figs. 6 and 7 some of these pencil sketches made by Fresquet on a reduced scale, as it were, in order to obtain and examine more quickly the composition effect required. Notice how these sketches have been made, using patches of pencil rather than lines so that all the potential and values of the subject can be assessed (Fig. 7).

«As you see», Fresquet stresses, «what I am most concerned with in this preliminary sketch is to fix the frame and examine the effects of light and shade in relation to the composition.»

★

Now we have a subject. Imagine that we are with Fresquet beside the road approaching a town in Tarragona. The houses are placed in line in the middle plane, separated from us by the green and earth of a few gardens and trees. It is half-past ten in the morning of a spring day. The sun lights up the scene, producing strong contrasts in the interplay of light and shade. If we half-close our eyes, we could say that there are only two colours: a light yellow in the sunlit areas and a bluish sienna in the shadows. The impression of volume is astonishing.

But wait: Fresquet has something to tell us:

«*Yes. Since we are now going to paint with every colour, I would like to explain in a practical manner the techniques always to be employed for painting a* dry *and* wet *watercolour.*»

«*Two styles, you mean?*»

«*That's right, and two very different methods which still form part of watercolour technique in the traditional and pure sense of the word.*»

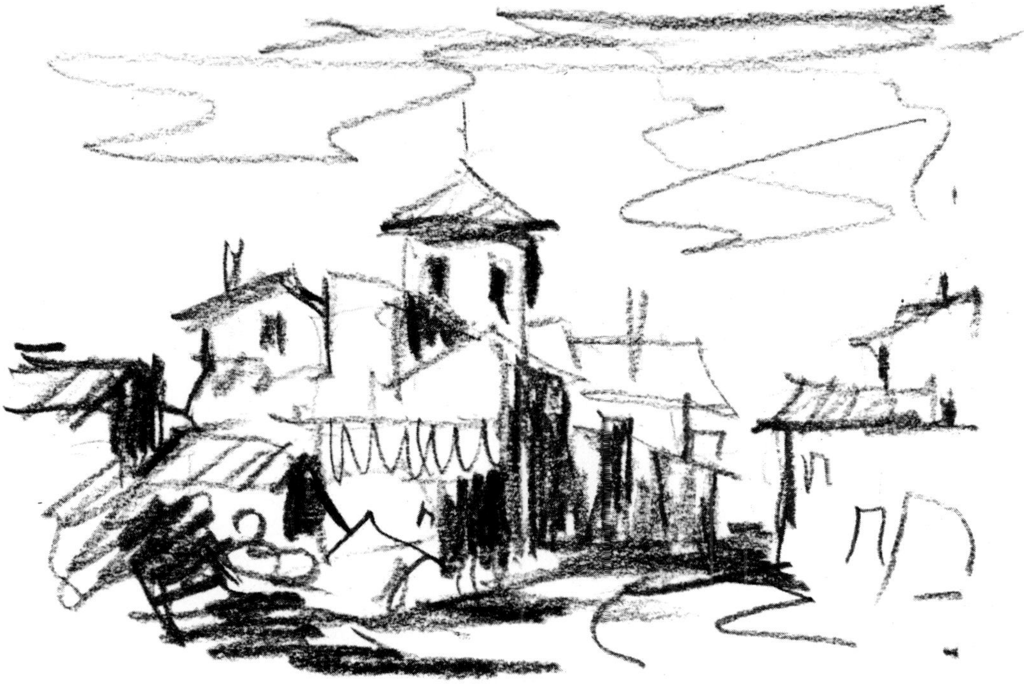

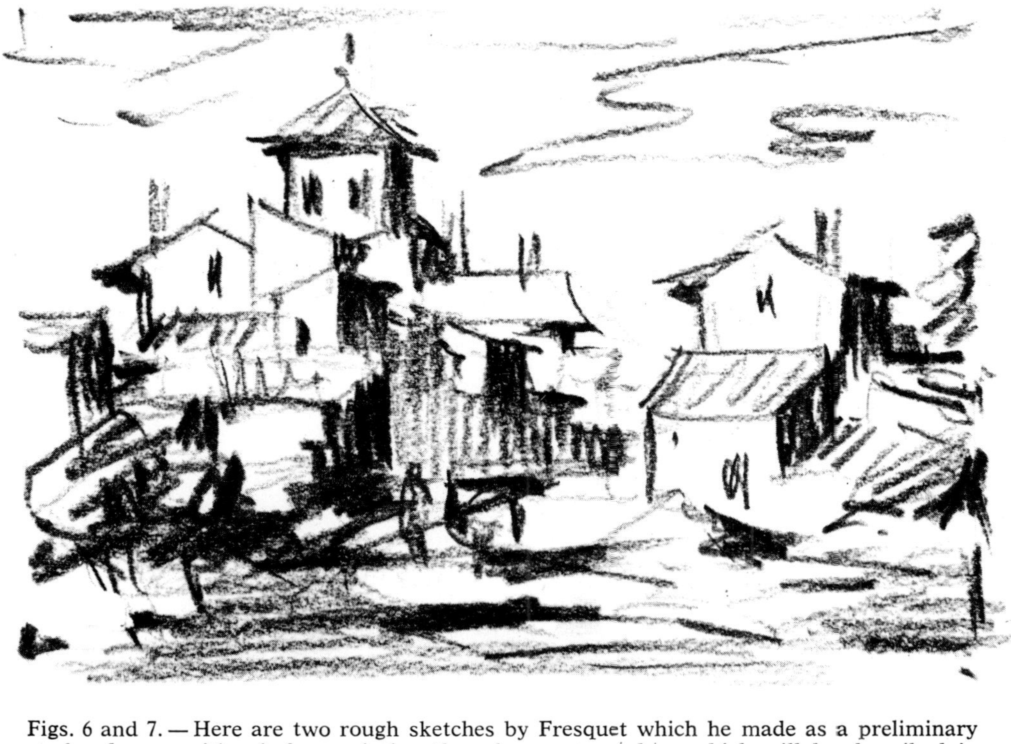

Figs. 6 and 7. — Here are two rough sketches by Fresquet which he made as a preliminary study of composition before painting the «dry» water colour which will be described in the following pages. In Fig. 6 the centre of interest (the road entering the town and forming a street between the houses) is too much off-centre.

THE TWO CLASSIC METHODS OF PAINTING IN WATERCOLOUR

«DRY» WATERCOLOUR AND «WET» WATERCOLOUR

You already know at least the theory of «wet» watercolour which is characterized basically by the fact that the paint is always put on wet paper which blends the colours and softens the outlines. You know too that with this method you must paint a succession of coats going upwards and outwards, which is done by applying light colours and tones and superimposing dark colours and tones. «Dry» watercolour is in some ways the exact opposite. The paint is usually laid on dry paper and dry coats and the darker colours and tones are applied first, so that...

But you will see what happens in practice when we watch and comment upon Guillermo Fresquet's work as he paints a «dry» watercolour.

FRESQUET PAINTS A «DRY» WATERCOLOUR

Wetting the paper to remove grease and gum

He begins by wetting the paper with a thick brush and clean water. Good: but I know what you are thinking...

But, whatever method you use, when painting watercolours you must always begin by wetting the paper in order to remove any grease or gum left on it and so prevent the colour running or the paper wrinkling under the effect of very wet washes, etc.

Fresquet now waits until the paper is completely dry and then begins by making a quick sketch with a lead pencil: this sketch is very simple and entirely two-dimensional, meaning that it contains no shadows nor grey or black areas.

While he is sketching in the shapes and profiles, a farmer goes by on the road leading a donkey. Fresquet watches them for a few moments and then more or less from memory draws the man and animal at the bend in the road. Then, as if reminded of something, he draws an indication of another figure more in the background.

«*What's that?*»

«*I should explain this. Whenever logical or possible, you should include in the picture one or more human figures, which besides providing colour — I shall paint the farmer with a touch of red and the background figure in blue — gives a feeling of life and reality, You might say, it is a little trick for bringing the picture alive. Apart from that, is it logical to paint a deserted town with no sign of human life?*»

Fresquet is a very clever painter. Notice, for example, this small detail and remember it: he has painted two figures and, almost instinctively, decided to use red for the first and blue for the more distant one. (You will see presently that, showing his skill and knowledge, he will paint the sacks on the donkey with a small but clearly visible touch of yellow. Can you guess why exactly he chooses yellow and red for the nearest figures and blue for the more distant one? Of course: because the two primaries bring forms closer, as it were, making them clearer and so placing them in the foreground while blue «removes» them. Remember this: it is important.

Red and yellow are «near» colours: blue is «distant».

«ALWAYS BEGIN BY PAINTING THE SKY»

«Is there any special reason?» you ask.

«Oh yes, several», replies Fresquet. First and foremost because when painting with watercolour, the clouds or the sky of any landscape have to be put in first, finished and done with: it must be left as the basis of the complete work. The reason for this strict rule is that a watercolour has to be considered as «an impressionistic painting, a work which captures a momentary appearance of the landscape», fresh, spontaneous and clean-cut, without any touching up. A landscape may include hills, houses, trees, etc. providing different planes and different colours as well as light and shade effects which produce different tones usually covering firmly delineated areas. These forms can and must be painted in sections, by drawing in shapes and superimposing and laying colours side by side. But the sky does not contain this diversity of forms and colours. The sky is a whole in itself. Even with the white and greys of the clouds, it has a uniformity of colour, a dominant blue, an expanse of blue which cannot be produced by small brush-strokes and layers of colour. We repeat and stress this rule:

The expanse of sky requires spontaneity and freshness.

When painting with watercolour, the sky of a landscape must be produced in its final form in the first place, without the need to go back and touch it up.

It is not easy to paint a wide expanse of cloudy sky under these conditions. Or rather, it requires a great deal of skill: you must know how to put on the water and paint in such a way as to prevent «breaks» and — even more difficult — you must have enough experience and courage to get the colour right first time, which is certainly far from easy when you remember that the rest of the picture is still white. The law of simultaneous contrasts plays a decisive role in this, namely that «a grey (or a blue, in this case) is stronger in proportion to the lightness of the surrounding tone.» You understand? When you have painted the sky while the rest of the paper is still unpainted, the sky appears to be very dark. But when you colour the remainder of the picture with tones and colours which are usually stronger than those of the sky, the sky then becomes lighter. It can turn out to be so light that it needs to be repainted!

Law of simultaneous contrasts.

So why run this risk? Why not paint the hills and houses first, giving them tone with a first coat (since we permit these forms to be repainted) and then paint the sky?

Well... you remember what I said just now: the sky has to be painted in one go and a clean result obtained, without any touching up or tricks — something which is not always successful. Can you imagine how annoyed an artist would be if after he has painted the roofs and walls of the houses, the colour of the ground and gardens, every roof with its own colour, every wall with its special tones, he then paints the sky and makes a mess of it!

No, the sky first, of course.

We can add other reasons: when you have painted the upper part of the picture, you can work and touch up the remainder without having to wait until the sky is completely dry; it is easier to harmonize the entire picture — despite what I have said about the law of simultaneous contrasts — since the sky is usually the largest area and when painted it governs the colours of the remainder.

Other reasons for painting the sky first.

(For this same reason, an oil-painter generally begins with the sky. But, when painting in oils which «cover» the underlying colours, another coat can be painted over the first, changing it, lightening or darkening it as required).

«Fine», Fresquet interrupts. «Nor must it be painted too dark With watercolour, the sky is done in a few moments. For this very reason, in order to paint it neatly, 'showing the water' as we artists say, leaving it fresh and spontaneous, we only have a few minutes. If you fail to hit the right colour immediately, you have no time to go over it again.»

«You will see this for yourselves», Fresquet adds, «notice how quickly it is done.»

FIRST STAGE (FIG. 8)

In his palette Fresquet mixes a neutral, slightly grey blue, using ultramarine, cobalt blue and a touch of sienna. He also prepares a grey from ultramarine and sienna... another grey which in addition to these two includes a touch of carmine. And he paints...

The paper is completely dry.

Fresquet loads his brush with water, takes blue and paints the upper left-hand section. The blue is rather light and not very wet. Immediately he takes up the grey. He paints below the blue. When the two colours meet, they blend together. He wipes his brush on the rag and applies it to the lower part of the grey area, soaking up colour and lightening it, while with a confident stroke of the brush he outlines the silhouette of the roofs. He now wants a rose-coloured shade: he takes a little red and mixes it with the grey on his palette. He gives a touch of it to the area on the horizon. The previous paint is still damp and the rose-grey spreads and blends with it.

Method used.

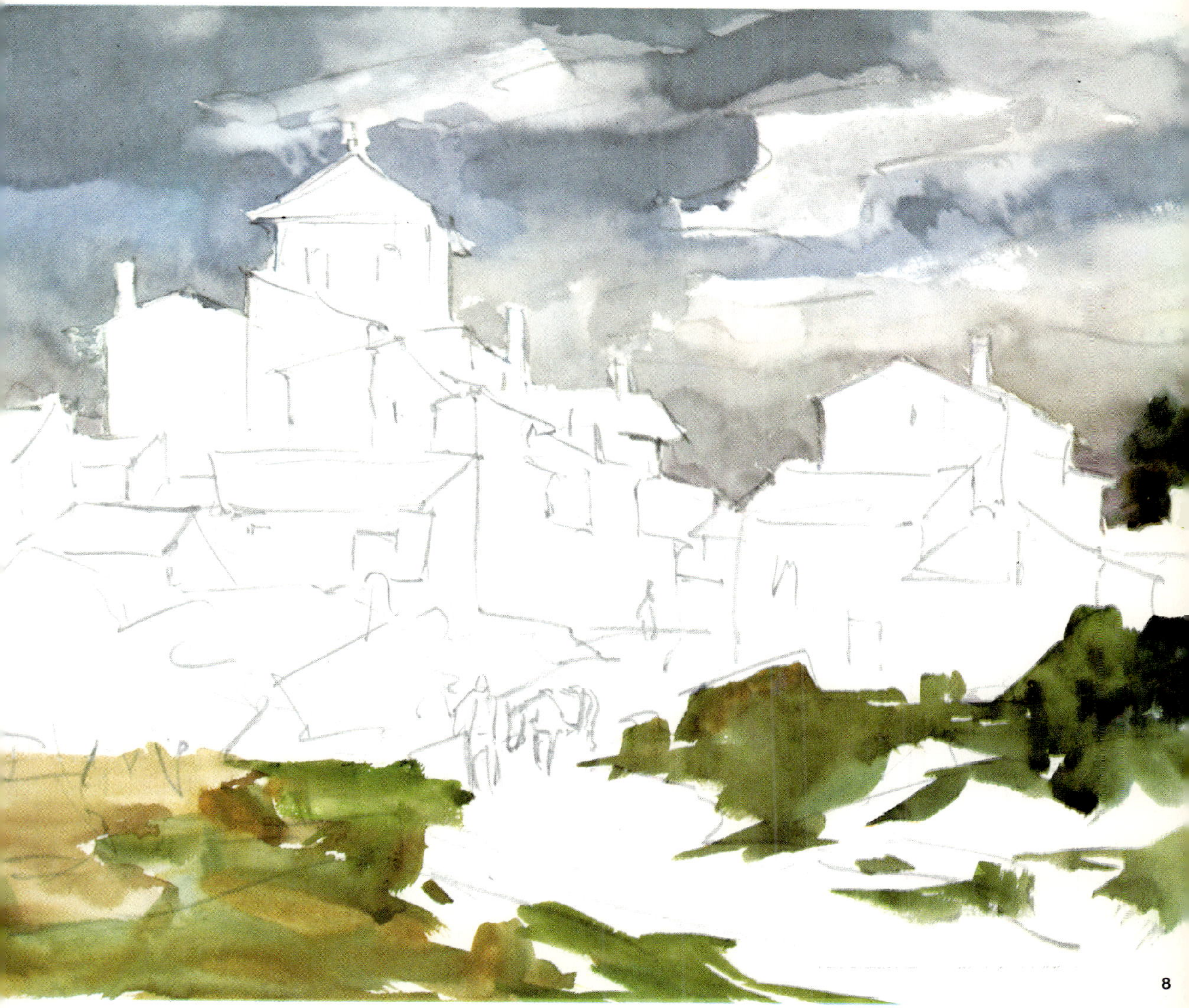

8

At the top, the first light blue is still slightly wet. Fresquet loads his brush with water and darker blue and paints over it. The darker blue spreads to form a patch... and goes on spreading as long as it remains wet. Some water has accumulated along its lower edge and when it dries it will form a slightly darker narrow strip (Fig. 8 illustrates these instructions and forms the first stage.)

The method used by Fresquet.

But Fresquet has not been slow in seeing what was happening to this edge of the blue patch. With his usual dexterity, he has been taking the blue wash towards the right over the tower, painting this new area on dry paper. First he marked out the form of that wide cloud drawn over the tower. See that white cloud marked out on dry paper — its whiteness is produced by the paper. What an astonishingly strange effect! Perhaps because Fresquet cleaned his brush and placed a brush-stroke of clean water inside the cloud, taking the water upwards, lightening the sky and shading the existing edge, which had formed a «break». On the other hand, he allowed the break to remain on the lower edge of the cloud.

Notice how the light blue which we mentioned earlier and which forms a «break» on the lower part of the cloud, has blended while wet with the grey of the horizon (on the right of the tower). Using the same method as before, Fresquet applies the dark blue in a wash which again spreads and blends with the light blue. But now, when it reaches the whiter area of the cloud, it forms a clean line, not touching the white or illuminated area of the cloud.

Do you see the method, this rather special way of «dry» painting? To sum up what has been done so far, we can say that Fresquet first applied the colour to dry paper but then, while the first was still wet, quickly painted another colour beside it, leaving them to blend together and shade under the effect of the moisture. When and where he thinks it necessary — following what the model «says» — Fresquet paints on a dry surface, deliberately forming a firm edge. In this way he is in fact using the two methods, both wet and dry, to produce either the blending or firm effects, as he thinks advisable. In practice, this is somewhat similar to painting a monochrome, by accumulating water at one point in order to re-work it before it can dry, and rationing it at another in order to outline and paint a firm shape by marking it out, etc.

«Dry» watercolour is easier than «wet».

You will realise immediately that this method calls for even more rapid working than wet watercolours, but the techniques are not the same. With the latter method, the wash must be even and flat, produced by continuous painting which does not allow you to go back over what you have done and which also requires constant wetness. Here, as you have seen, you can go back, adding a stronger colour, soaking up, and so on. «Breaks» are comparatively important since they are called for in many places. With «wet» watercolour, a «break» means that you have to begin all over again.

Weak and strong outlines.

To go back to Fresquet's work, on the right side of the horizon you will notice the patch of dark green representing some trees behind the houses. See how the edge of these trees is diluted with the greyish colour of the sky as a result of both colours blending when wet. Note that Fresquet has produced this effect in these trees while firmly delineating the profile of the houses. This is logical: we can assume that these trees are situated in a more distant ground than the houses and form part of the background. So it is quite correct to weaken these outlines and thus create the sense of space between the planes of the houses and trees. This induces us to give the following rule:

When painting «dry» watercolours, the outlines in the more distant grounds must be formed by the «wet» method in order to produce the effect of space and intervening atmosphere.

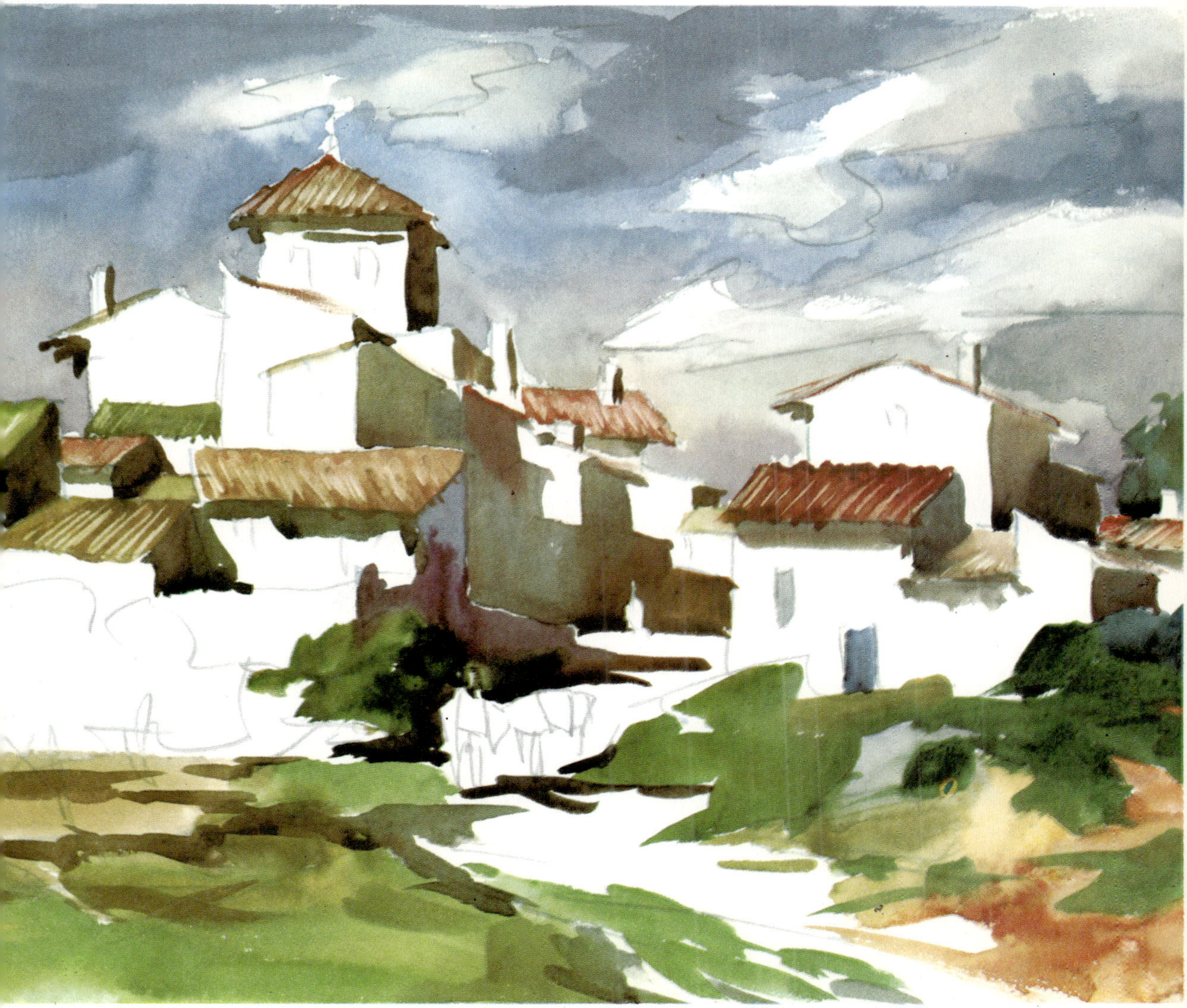

To complete this first stage, Fresquet dry-paints the greens and siennas of the earth, but nevertheless using the «wet» method at various points.

SECOND STAGE (FIG. 9)

Study carefully Fig. 9. Its shows the characteristic difference of the method we are studying: this is that, when the sky is finished, the artist turns to the darker parts of the subject and paints the strong colours, leaving out the medium and light shades. This system is so important that it must be emphasized:

> **The technique of «dry» watercolours is characterised by the fact that the darker areas of the subject are painted first (dark shadows and strong colours), leaving out the white highlights.**

A more dramatic effect, isn't it? and how convenient to be able to paint in this way, drawing, outlining and filling in the volume of the objects... and also being able to go back and touch up if necessary with a new coat, strengthening or giving tone to the colours.

A method which obeys the above formula is of course bound to produce a final powerful picture with strong contrasts and great effect, as we can see. This brings us to a new aspect:

«Dry» watercolour is suitable for painting subjects or models wich offer wide contrasts. As a classic model, we can mention a landscape in strong sunlight.

But notice how carefully Fresquet has marked out the forms which are in medium or light colours: for example, the small figure in the background, the chimneys, etc.

Notice too how in this second stage Fresquet has painted the roofs, each having the original colour of the subject. (Not by «mass-producing» them in just one colour, as some inexperienced amateurs would do...) He has reproduced the shapes of the roofs by means of light lines or strokes which have been «revealed» with the tip of an old brush-handle, as we explained earlier.

Roofs drawn with the tip of a brush-handle.

THIRD AND LAST STAGE (FIG. 10)

At this stage, Fresquet first paints the lighter areas, the broad colour washes which correspond to the large, more illuminated areas: the light road, the creamy-yellow colour which lights most of the houses, etc. Fresquet paints these light areas with long brush-strokes without bothering too much whether they go over the lines. When he comes to areas which may subsequently have to be painted in a darker colour (for instance, the walls and earth on the left where he will later paint two or three trees), he paints it entirely in the light colour.

Third stage: First, light colours on the dark which are now dry.

This is a job with which Fresquet takes extreme care, so as not to allow these light washes to intrude upon the dark colours of the shadows already painted. These dark colours are of course dry. So you must remember that if these very wet washes touched them, they would produce patches and bad colouring which would show up the artist's lack of skill. The same applies to occasional strokes with a brush loaded with water or light washes which can cause very obvious patches similar to those produced intentionally by the soaking up method.

In these light colours — and in fact in all the colours — how concerned Fresquet is to obtain colour differentiation which enriches the picture. Study carefully each of the areas of colour forming the sunlit walls, and see how in some there is a yellow tinge and in others a rose, etc. See how there are even slight differences in shade in each surface, subtle but obvious touches of colour which animate and heighten the

Artistic variations and shades of colour.

artistic quality of the picture. Notice, for instance, the number of fine shades obtained in the luminous colouring of the road.

Now the intermediate tones and colours.

Fresquet continues by painting the intermediate tones, such as the sienna on the front wall of the house on the right. Here, and on some of the other houses, he surely applied these intermediate colours while the previous light colour was still wet. That is what he is doing now with the trees on the left, almost in the foreground, which are painted entirely with the «wet» watercolour method, first putting on that light green and then, while it is still wet, applying the darker green for the areas in shadow.

Next he paints the figures, doors and windows and the horizontal shadows in the foreground which are produced by thick rapid strokes.

Final touches.

Finally, the finishing touches consist firstly of balancing some values, strengthening colours at some points and soaking up and weakening others... For instance, look at that kind of vertical light strip in the shadow of the houses along the street just above the man and donkey. Have you found it? Look at this area in Fig. 9. If you compare the two figures, you can see that in the first one Fresquet did not allow for the need for contrast which detaches the nearest house from the more distant one, forming a space between the two (this was overlooked partially because the subject did not produce this effect very clearly). However, Fresquet solves the problem quite easily by removing colour with his wet brush, using the method explained earlier.

Making white lines.

All we need do now is to see how Fresquet obtains small white lines with the end of the brush and his fingernail, making the strokes on the grass in the foreground —using his brush— or the kind of thick lines on the right edge of the road —in yellow, using his fingernail—. Notice too the two small light vertical lines, representing windows in the shadowed houses along the street.

To sum up this «dry» watercolour method, I shall now pick out the salient features:

1. Paint and finish the sky.

2. «Dry» paint the darker areas (shadows and strong colours, etc.) leaving out the white highlights.

5. Wait until the entire picture is dry and colour the lighter areas, representing the more luminous parts.

4. «Dry» or «wet» paint the intermediate tones and colours, whichever is most suitable.

5. Paint small dark details.

6. Balance tones and colours, strengthening or soaking up, make the small white lines, etc. (finishing touches).

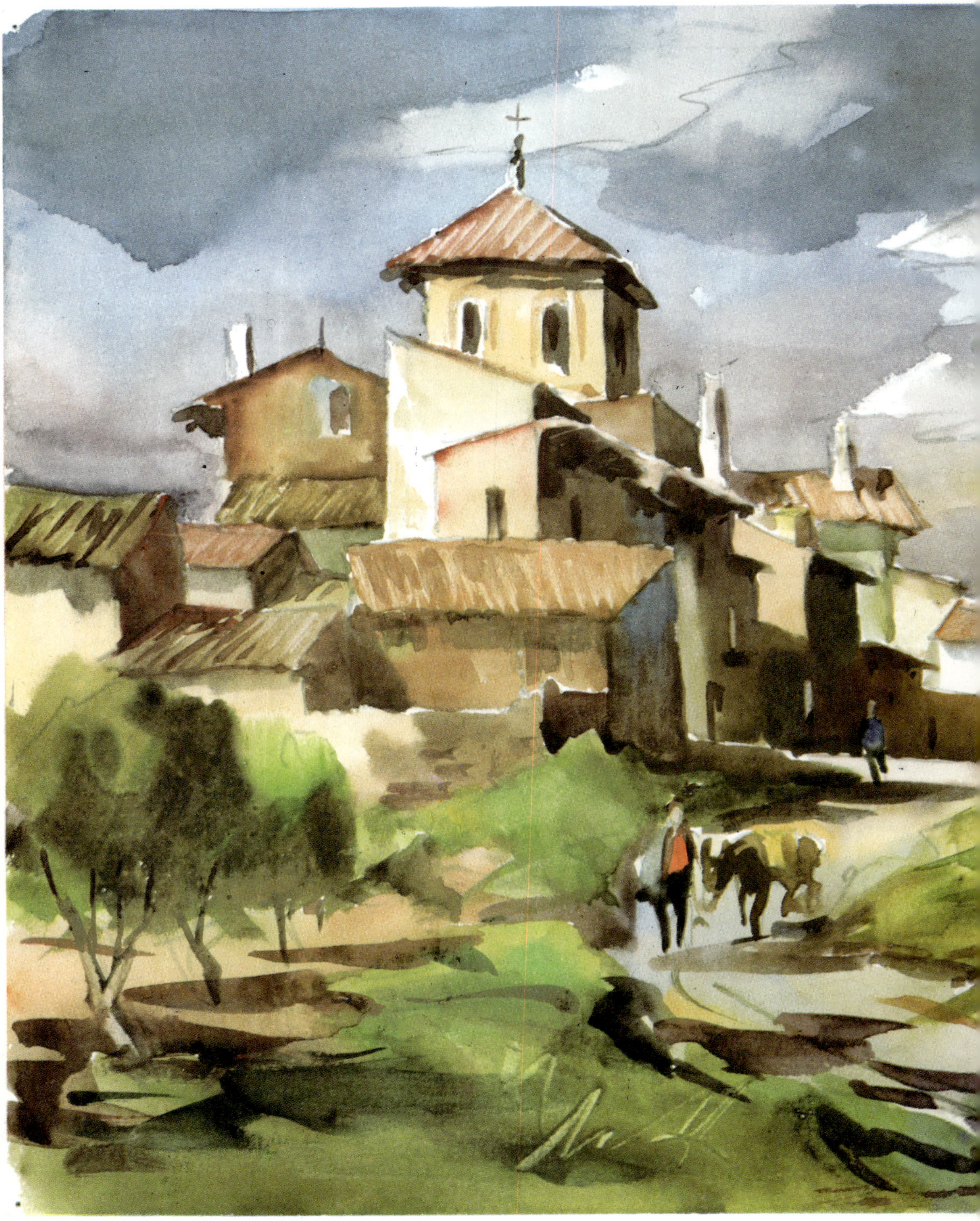

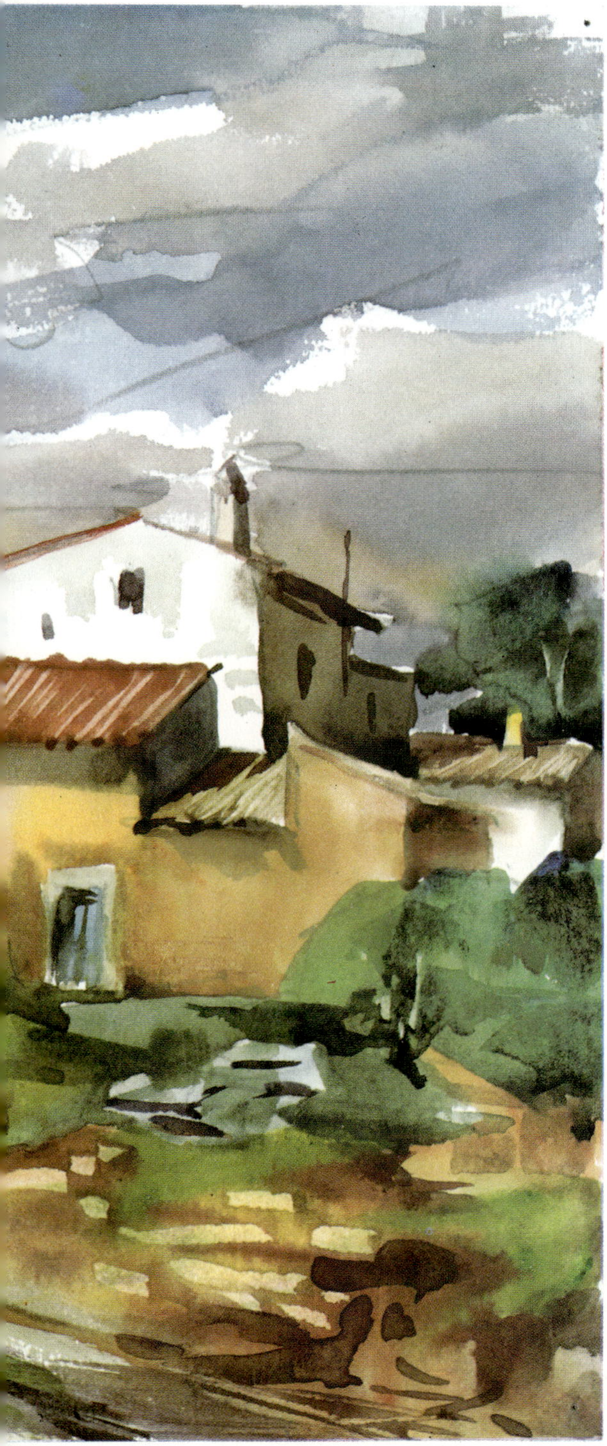

93

Fig. 10. — The final result obtained by Guillermo Fresquet for the watercolour specially painted for the Parramon Institute as part of these instructions in the «dry» technique. The original painting is slightly larger than here (25 x 32 cm.).

FRESQUET PAINTS A «WET» WATERCOLOUR

Now we come to another technique and another subject. This time somewhere not far from Barcelona, near San Baudilio de Llobregat, on a cloudy day: one of those afternoons following a rainy morning with the ground and fields still wet, when the sun suddenly breaks through the clouds, creating a wonderful symphony of light and colour.

Fresquet called me that midday:

«*Parramon! It's stopped raining and is cloudy but the sun seems about to come out. Do you think we should try...?*»

And there we were: Fresquet jumped at it when he found it before on a similar afternoon driving along this road. «And then it was even better», he says. «In the background there was a superb golden light». Like every artist, Fresquet talks in very visual terms. Perhaps he was right but, like me, he realises that once you have seen something of this kind, memory and imagination make it into something sublime, «golden», more so than it actually is.

Even without these comments, the subject is, of course, superb. Look at the finished work in Fig. 13.

FIRST THE SKY... AND IN THIS CASE THE TREETOPS

But wait; as before, first you must wet the paper because of the grease and gum. Then sketch in the subject with a few lines, just enough to site the objects (You can see how confidently Fresquet draws). There was certainly no preliminary sketch in this case. Fresquet says that he could remember the frame, contrasts, colouring, composition and — no need to tell you! — the light. Speaking of composition, as well as an original foreground — that empty space between us and the nearest trees does not conform to the classic idea of a foreground —notice the unity and order produced by the diagonal composition and the effect of variety caused by the virtually oblique line of perspective formed by the road and the line of trees.

Description of the subject: Notice the diagonal composition.

Begin the painting with the sky, including the treetops, using the «wet» watercolour method.

FIRST STAGE (FIG. 11)

The first essential stage when using the «wet» watercolour method:

FIRST WET THE PAPER SO THAT YOU WILL START PAINTING ON A WET SURFACE

«It should not be too wet», Fresquet emphasizes. «If you hold the paper at an angle so that the light shines along it, the water itself should

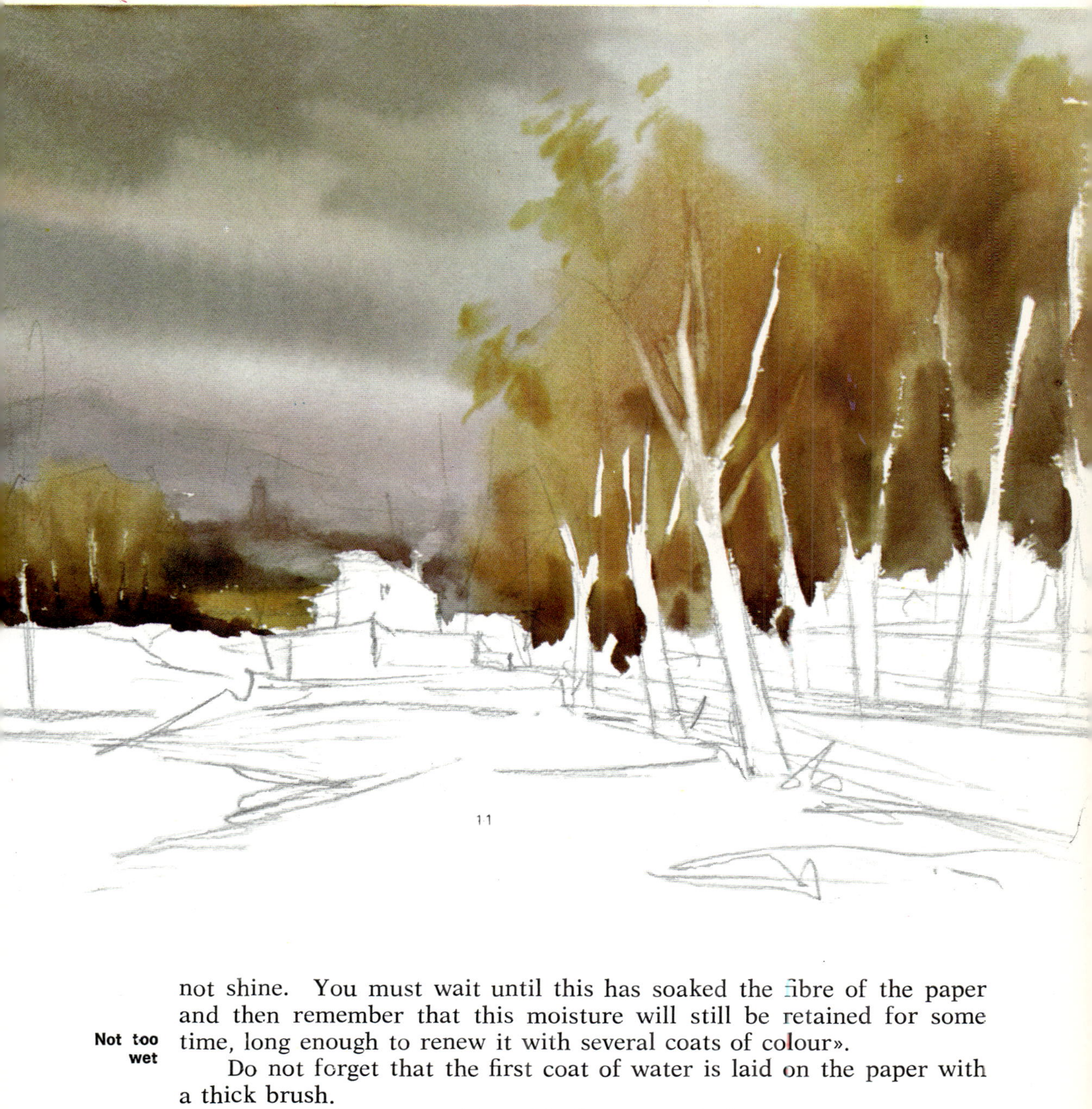

11

not shine. You must wait until this has soaked the fibre of the paper and then remember that this moisture will still be retained for some time, long enough to renew it with several coats of colour».

Not too wet

Do not forget that the first coat of water is laid on the paper with a thick brush.

Fresquet is now applying this first coat of clean water. He is particularly careful to leave out the white areas formed by the tree-trunks, as well as all the lower section corresponding to the foreground and middle plane. Speaking of planes, notice how Fresquet has preferred to fix the horizontal line forming the boundary of the green field behind the shed, nearer and lower than the actual horizon. He does this so that the real horizon and far distance can be blurred using the «wet» watercolour technique, and thus the contours are dissolved, creating a greater sense of distance and depth.

Dissolving the far distance.

But on the right he makes the «break» above the horizon, forming the lower edge of the trees' foliage, since he feels that this is closer and can be made more concrete.

The lesson to be drawn from this is important: it shows us how the far distance must always be dissolved to contrast with the solid forms with their varying degrees of emphasis in the middle and foregrounds

But Fresquet is starting to paint, so let's get back to the picture. He begins in the upper left-hand corner of the sky, applying a light warm grey to the wet surface. He spreads this first grey towards the right, diluting it with more water as it approaches the treetops. He also paints this area, shading in the centre with clean water. He then spreads this light grey downwards and when it becomes close to the real horizon, he adds a very small amount of carmine. He returns to the upper left-hand section and applies a slightly rose-coloured but nevertheless light grey.

Painting the sky.

He next mixes a darker grey and paints the large threatening dark clouds with wide brush-strokes. Aided by the moisture, the colour slowly spreads, smoothly and evenly. Fresquet helps by soaking the colour wherever it accumulates and adding colour in very light touches where necessary...

«*It is better to leave it,*» he says, «*under no circumstances should you stop, wasting time on the sky.*»

He then paints that little hill with the castle using ultramarine blue, sienna, carmine..., he soaks up colour from the upper section, adds a brown with a stronger carmine tinge.

With astonishing speed he mixes the ochre of the trees from sienna and a little green, neutralising it with red or carmine when he wants a rose-tinted ochre, or with ultramarine blue when he paints the greens with a khaki tint. He applies the same range of colour to the trees on the left up to the horizon.

...the trees.

On the few occasions when, due to dryness, he realises that a «break» could occur, he quickly adds clean water, just enough to blend the colours.

Fresquet stresses the method of painting dark tones on light colours. For instance, in the large area of foliage on the right, he begins by painting with the lighter rose-tinted ochre, adding new darker coats and colours until he obtains the result shown in Fig. 11.

Dark tones on light tones.

SECOND STAGE (FIG. 12)

Using the same methods as before, Fresquet now turns to the ground, fields, the grey strip of the road, etc. Again he begins by wetting the paper with clean water, leaving out the whole of the shed and the area forming the river, as well as the tree-trunks.

Painting the ground.

Notice how in the land and fields, some colours have been blended with others before the final phase, so that it is perfectly possible to correct, remove and add colours, etc. while the paper remains wet.

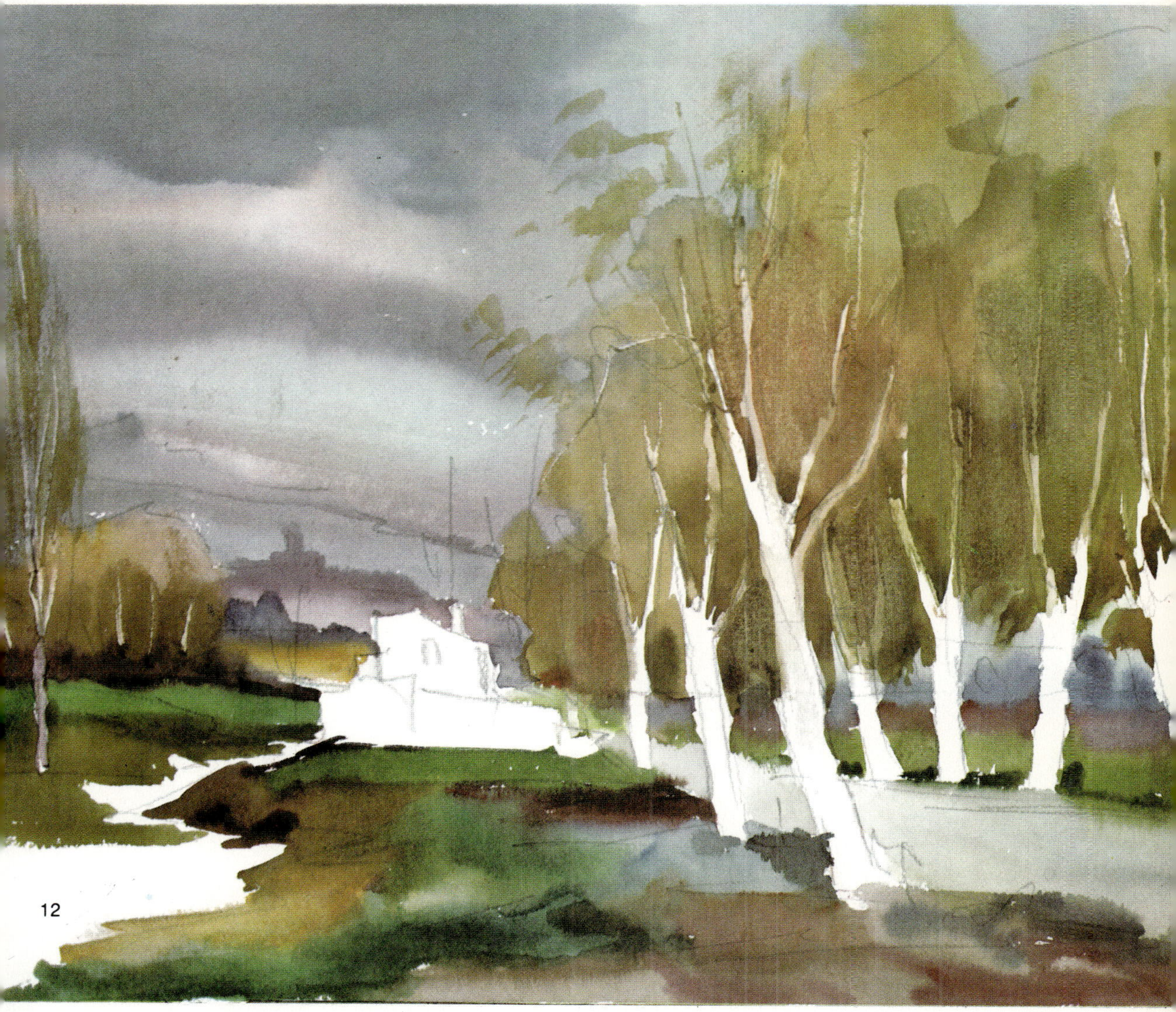

12

THIRD AND LAST STAGE (FIG. 13)

We shall now discuss how Fresquet paints water and reflections, expanding these instructions to cover more specific and wider applications than here; for instance, harbour scenes with boats at anchor.

HOW TO PAINT WATER AND ITS REFLECTIONS

First a transparent wash reflecting the colour of the sky.

Fresquet explains that he makes a rule of first applying an overall very light wash, which as it becomes wet, reflects the colour of the sky. If the subject requires it, he leaves out a brilliant, completely white area, even when he finds that these areas are only produced when the sunlight forms whitecaps on the water along our line of vision. This is rather rare since it is not advisable to paint with such light conditions. If necessary these pure white areas can be produced by reflections of white boats under sunlight.

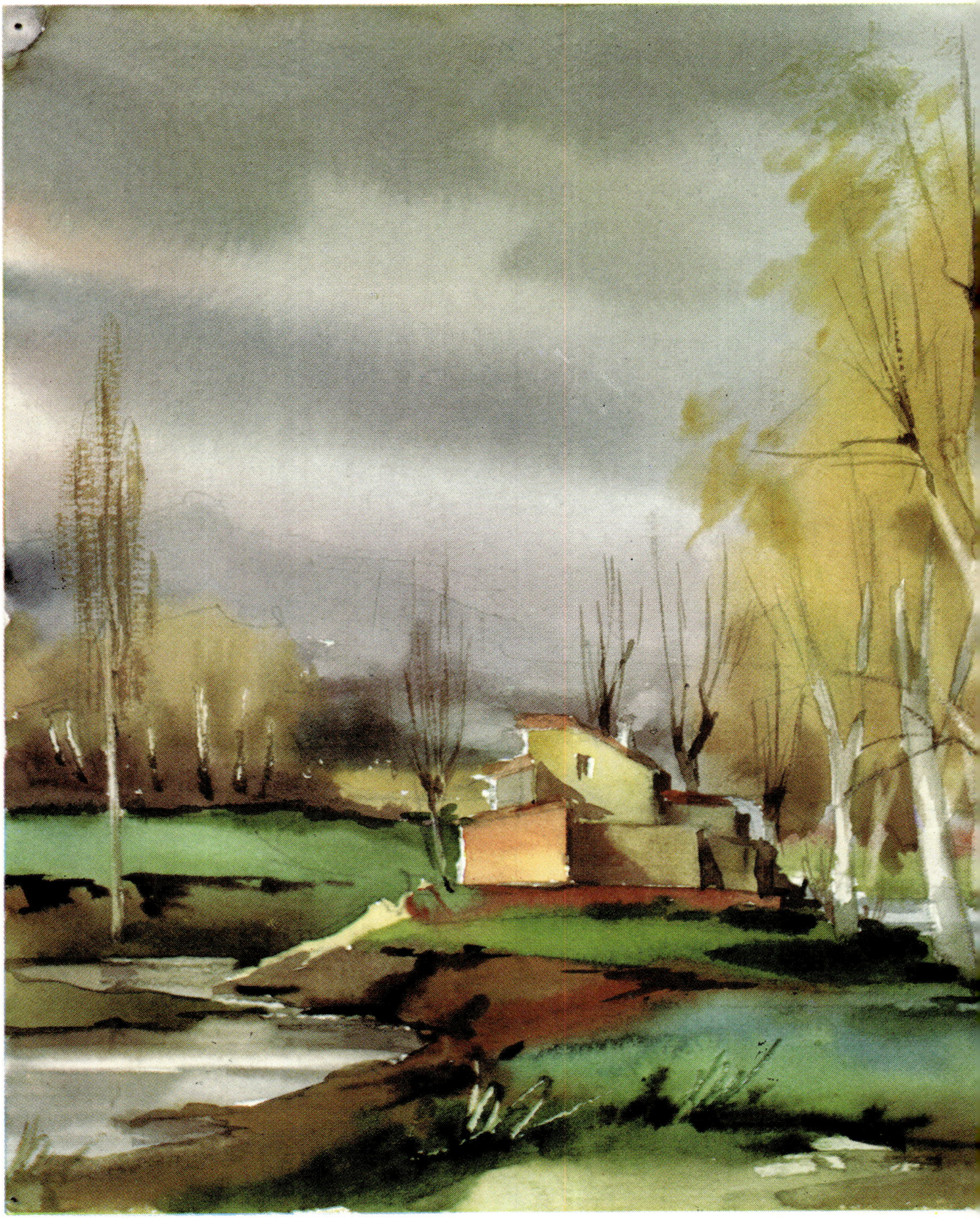

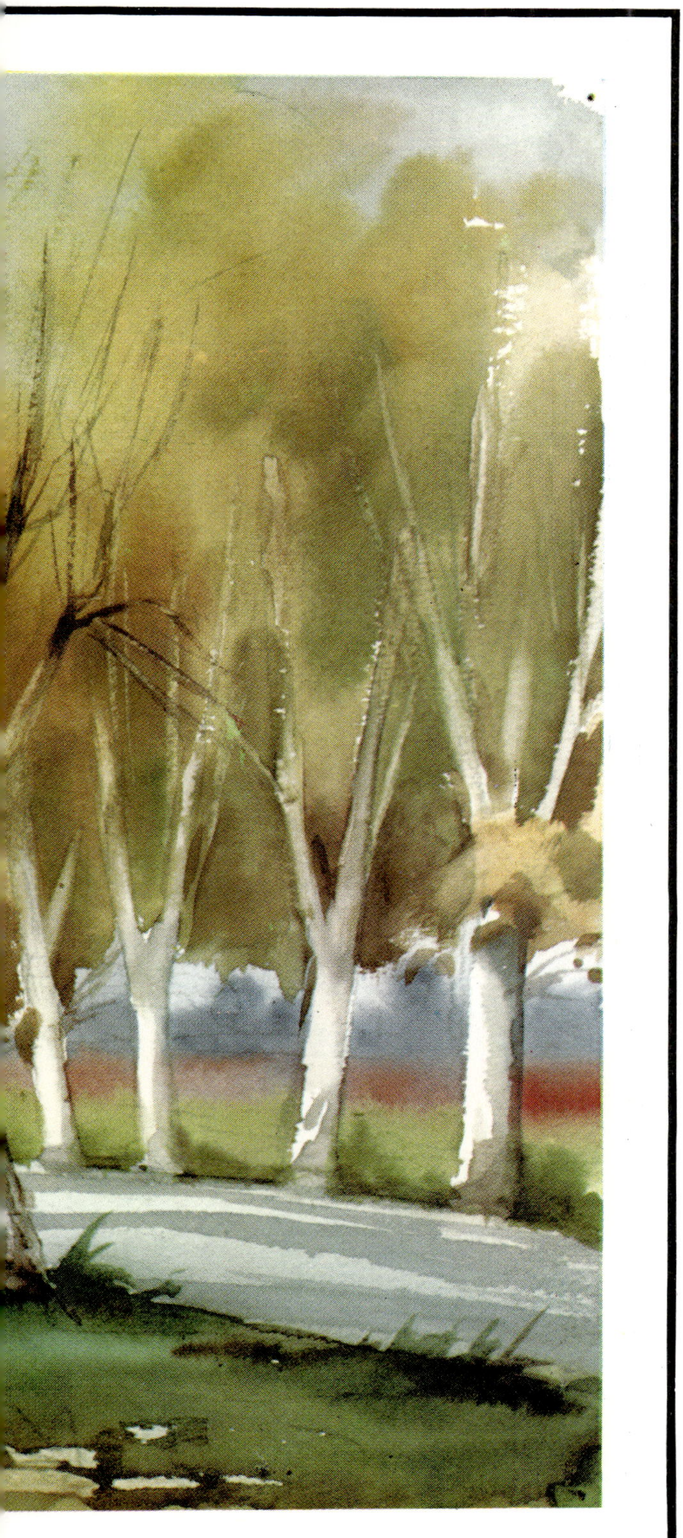

Fig. 13. — This is the final «wet» watercolour obtained by Guillermo Fresquet, specially painted as an example of this classic watercolour technique. The exact measurements of the original are 25 x 32 cm.

While the first light coat reflecting the sky is still wet —«I have painted blue skies, grey skies and even gold and yellow skies», he says, — Fresquet applies the dark tones of the forms reflected in the water. When painting these tones, Fresquet «draws», that is to say he produces concrete forms following the model· As a last resort, Fresquet finds no difficulty in obtaining white areas which he has been unable to leave out in advance. «When you are using good class paper, you can soak up more colour than you would think, leaving almost pure white areas. It is also very troublesome when you realise that, besides having to leave out all shapes and sizes of white areas, you must make a thousand little strokes to paint the dark forms reflected in the water, without in the end producing an even overall result. I advise an amateur to use both methods, marking out the «artificial» white areas in advance and

Then the dark colours reflected in the water

White areas can be obtained by soaking up, using the brush as a sponge.

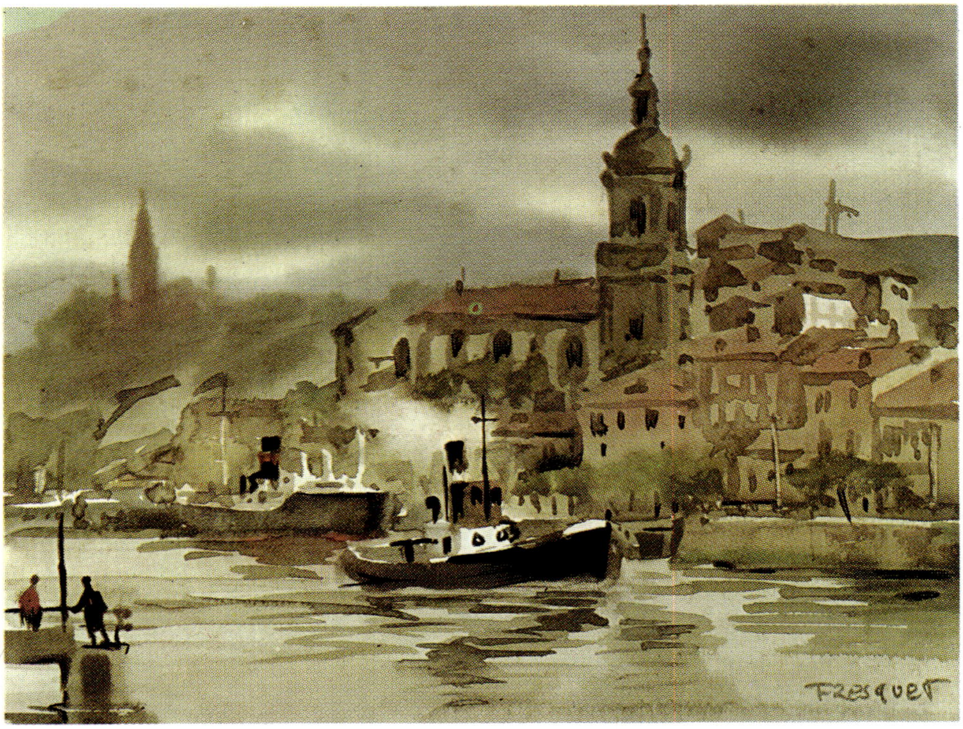

14

also soaking up colour with the brush in order to «reveal» them after painting. In this way you will get a less clear-cut and more 'real' finish. However, I repeat that very obvious highlights or strong white areas must be marked out in advance.»

In the water shown in our landscape, the white reflection of the horizontal strip has been obtained by soaking up colour with the brush.

FINISHING TOUCHES

Getting back to our main subject, Fresquet paints a coat of rather dirty cream on the tree-trunks towards the background in order to make them more distant. Then he produces the trunks' cylindrical form by applying burnt grey. As a special touch he lets white paper show through on the two nearest trunks, forming the highlights.

The vertical lines like thin branches on the nearest trees are made by scratching with the tip of the brush-handle.

To finish off the nearest areas of the ground, Fresquet uses a method which is very similar to «dry» watercolours. He begins by wetting the areas with clean water (without rubbing or scraping with the brush). When they are almost completely dry, he paints them over with darker colours.

In the final stage, some parts are «dry»-painted.

He first uses the «dry» method for painting the overall light tones of the shed and immediately brings out the volume with dark tones applied while the previous coats are wet. Fresquet felt it necessary to leave out those thin strips of white on the left face of the shed which give the building greater volume and distinguish it more clearly from the back-ground with its blended values.

Tricks of the trade.

Finally, painting on dry coats, Fresquet marks in the very small shapes such as the thin tree-trunks, the shadows of the trees on the road, the blades of grass, lines or strips separating the fields, etc. In some cases, such as the tall bare trees behind the shed. Fresquet applies too dark a tone, whether intentionally or not. His method could not be easier — and it is worth remembering this: he simply runs a finger over it in the direction of the line (vertical, in this case) and this removes some of the colour, producing the tone required.

All that remains is to balance some of the colours, adding or removing them, to «reveal» a white area by means of his fingernail, etc.

★

The job is finished. Let's go back to Barcelona. Tomorrow we have arranged to go to Barcelona Port. Fresquet will paint a large watercolour for us.

The picture between these pages is a full-scale reproduction of «Barcelona Port» painted specially for the Parramon Institute by Guillermo Fresquet. It has been printed by photo-litho offset on special Torras offset paper. This is the picture to be used as a model for the final, comprehensive exercise of these instructions on watercolour. Simply remove it and place it in front of you, following the instructions given on page 104.

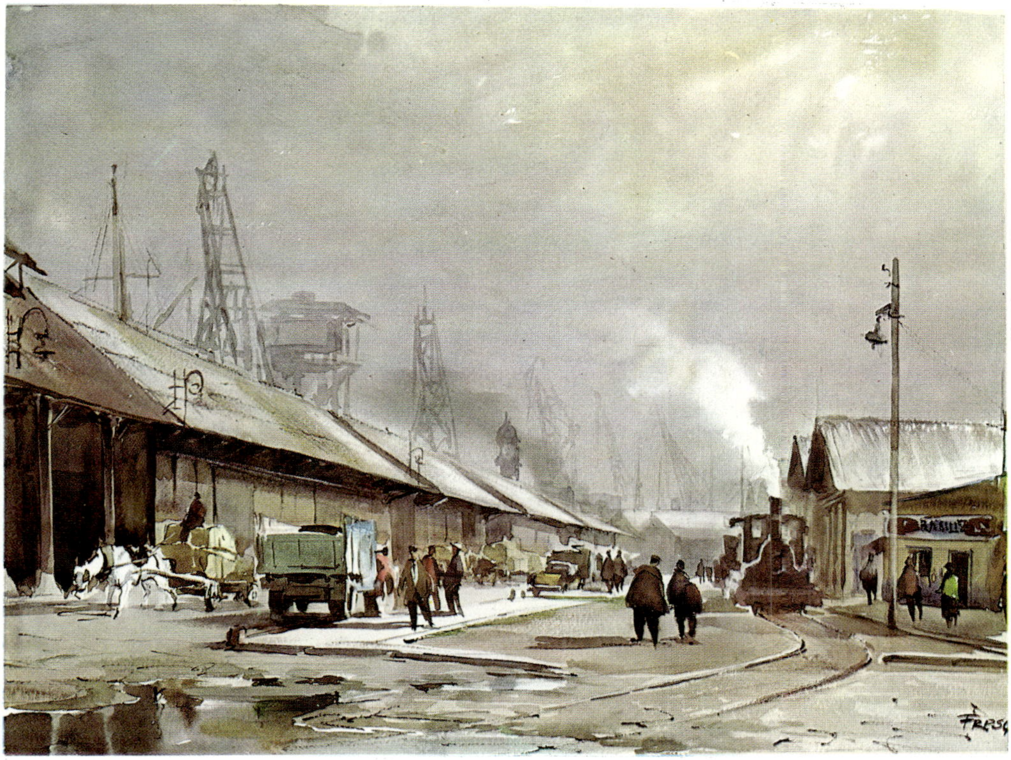

Now for the final test: using every colour, you are going to paint Guillermo Fresquet's watercolour «Barcelona Port» reproduced in the attached picture.

Look at the model, a full-colour, full-scale reproduction of the original on special offset paper for photo-litho offset. Have you the courage? Can't you imagine it painted by yourself, framed and hung on your wall?

To help you we have shown the first and second stages of this painting on pages 108-109 and 112-113, so that you can more easily and clearly see how it developed. Look at those pictures as well, study them, noting the procedure employed by Fresquet.

So, the exercise is «simply» to copy another artist's work. But besides the lessons learnt from copying an expert's work–remember that every great artist began «by drinking from the fountain of famous masters» as Leonardo da Vinci himself said; remember that Velasquez and Fortuny, to name only two great examples, went to Rome to paint and study in the museums there, copying famous pictures— and also, besides the fact that you will have practical experience of the composition, technique and colouring of an expert watercolour artist, this exercise will give you a marvellous opportunity to follow step by step the path of an expert, to see and listen to his advice almost as if he were beside you, guiding your hand.

So please make this «simple» copy with as much enthusiasm and pleasure as you would bring to your own work and with the same hopes, bearing in mind that this is an essential step towards working on your own.

Chance to follow an artist's work step by step.

Did I say this copy was «simple?» Not really, as you will see:

GENERAL INSTRUCTIONS

1. Make all your preparations with great care. Do not omit any of the materials and equipment: really get ready to do a perfect job. Work with a wooden board or a panel which is large enough to hold the paper easily, fixing it with plenty of drawing-pins in order to prevent subsequent wrinkles caused by the moisture. Have a pot or jar available big enough to hold the water: find a piece of smooth rag, old but clean, which will easily absorb the water and colour from the brushes when you use it for drying... Spend a little time on arranging your work-table: do it carefully, since this exercise is really important.

The exercise is important. Take care with your preparations.

2. Place some sort of stand on the table so that you can set out and see the models for the first and second stages. Ideally, the large model, that is the printed copy of the final work, should be pinned to the wall in front or beside you. In this way you will be able to see in one glance all the colouring used in the first and second stages and the final result.

Let's formulate a rule from this:

To study the colours properly, it is best to examine simultaneously all the reproductions of the subject in this book, corresponding to the first and second stages and, at the same time, the model of the finished work.

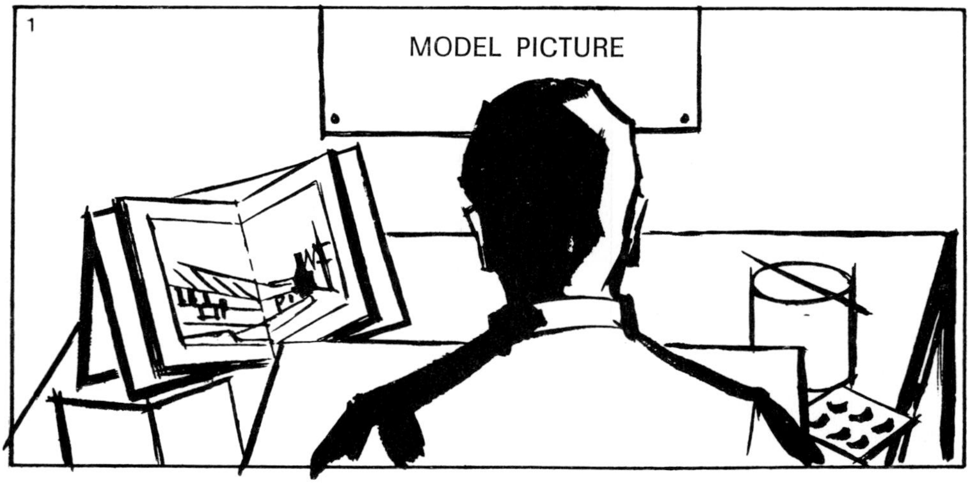

3. The original size of Fresquet's painting is 33.5 x 48 cm. So first obtain a sheet at least the same size. To make your work easier, we advise you to draw a rectangle of 33.5 x 48 cm. in the centre of it: when you have done this, cut off the surplus edge leaving a margin of some three-quarters of an inch all round.

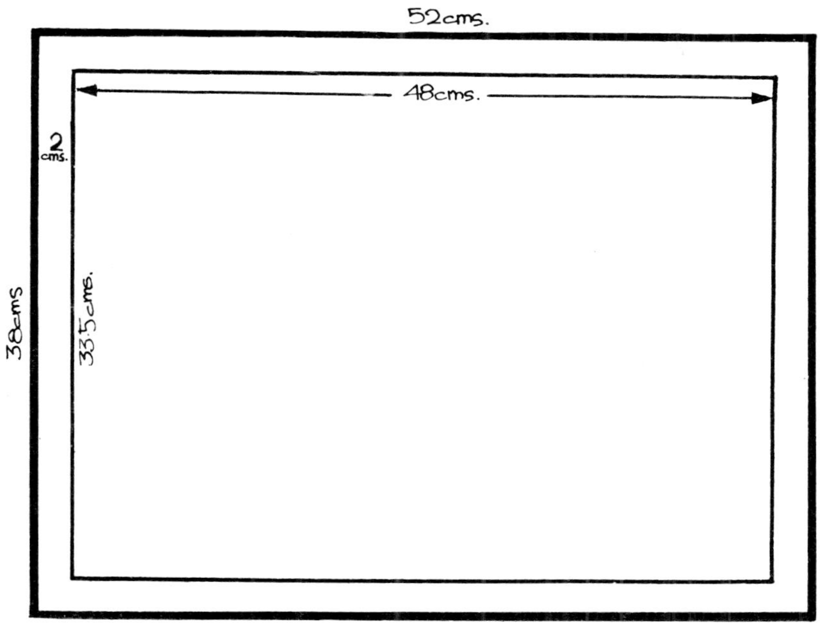

This three-quarters of an inch is to be used for fastening the paper with drawing-pins... or with strips of gummed paper, using the method described on page 17.

Daylight is best.

4. This exercice can be done either in daylight or artifical light. But, to enable you to gain a better appreciation of the colours, we recommend you to work in daylight.

FIRST STEP: THE SQUARING METHOD

Study Fresquet's pencil sketch.

5. Fig. 3 shows a reduced version of the original pencil sketch which Fresquet has done as part of this composition stage. Look at this drawing and see its fluency and astonishing confidence gained from hundreds of sketches and hundreds of drawings —you learn to draw by drawing. Learn from it: notice how it is built up from clear, unfussy lines without resorting to two or three lines where one will do. You must work like this— or at least try to.

6. Now we are going to paint a copy using really professional methods, just as if we were going to a museum to copy a picture. As you know, when doing this the professional artist does not waste time by relying solely on his eyes, working directly from the picture in the classic

and only way of drawing from nature. He does not waste one of his sessions in the museum standing before the picture simply in order to draw the subject. He stays at home and works from a good reproduction, squaring it and making the drawing from the actual surface of the copy by means of the squaring method. This is obviously just as good as getting the original drawing from the artist who painted it... But this is what we do have! Even in this first stage we can make an accurate copy of Fresquet's painting. This will be our first step:

Copying in museums

Square off Fig. 3 — Fresquet's drawing — and transfer an enlarged version of it to the drawing-paper, reproducing it in its original size.

7. We must therefore make an accurate, identical drawing of Fresquet's own drawing but, of course, enlarging it to the size of the original, that is 33.5 x 48 cm.

Enlarging by squaring off.

8. I must stress the importance of this drawing being an exact copy, an identical and precise reproduction of each area, line and plane. By doing this you will have the chance to see how a real professional goes about it. You will realise, for instance, that in his drawing Fresquet does not include every detail of the original subject: you will see that professionals sketch in the forms in only enough detail to enable them to finish and adapt them as they paint. With this knowledge, you will see the need to work spontaneously from the very beginning and not bother with minor finicky touches.

Make an exact copy of this drawing.

9. So you must never adopt an over-fussy attitude —the disordered, anxious manner of the clumsy amateur. Keep this firmly in mind:

But be careful with composition.

At this stage, your exercise must not contain faults in composition, position and proportions.

Even when the basic drawing is finished in keeping with Fresquet's outline, you can still adjust part of the sketch, adding more detailed items such as the cranes which appear above the buildings on the left, or angles and profiles of these buildings or others, etc... (See these extra details in the finished model).

Where necessary add structural details.

FIRST STAGE: PAINTING THE SKY AND GENERAL TONES (pp. 108-109)

10. Before going any further, it is necessary to decide which method is to be used for this watercolour, that is to say whether the style and technique are to be «dry» or «wet» watercolour.

The answer is: «wet» watercolour... but not as a hard and fast rule, since many areas have to be «dry»-painted. Both methods are to be used, producing a highly classical result. You can see this for yourself if you study carefully the fullsize model.

«Wet» method, but sometimes the «dry» technique.

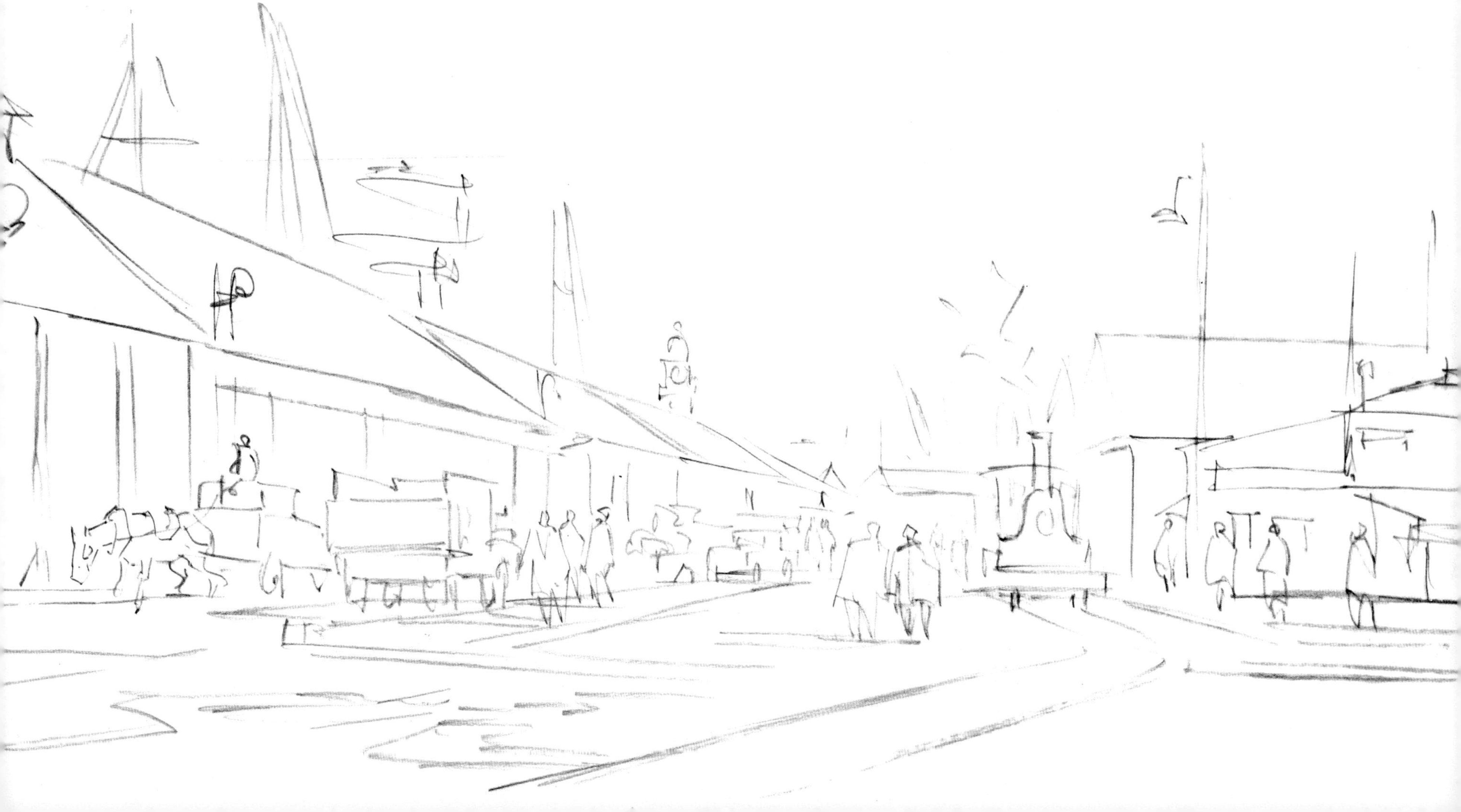

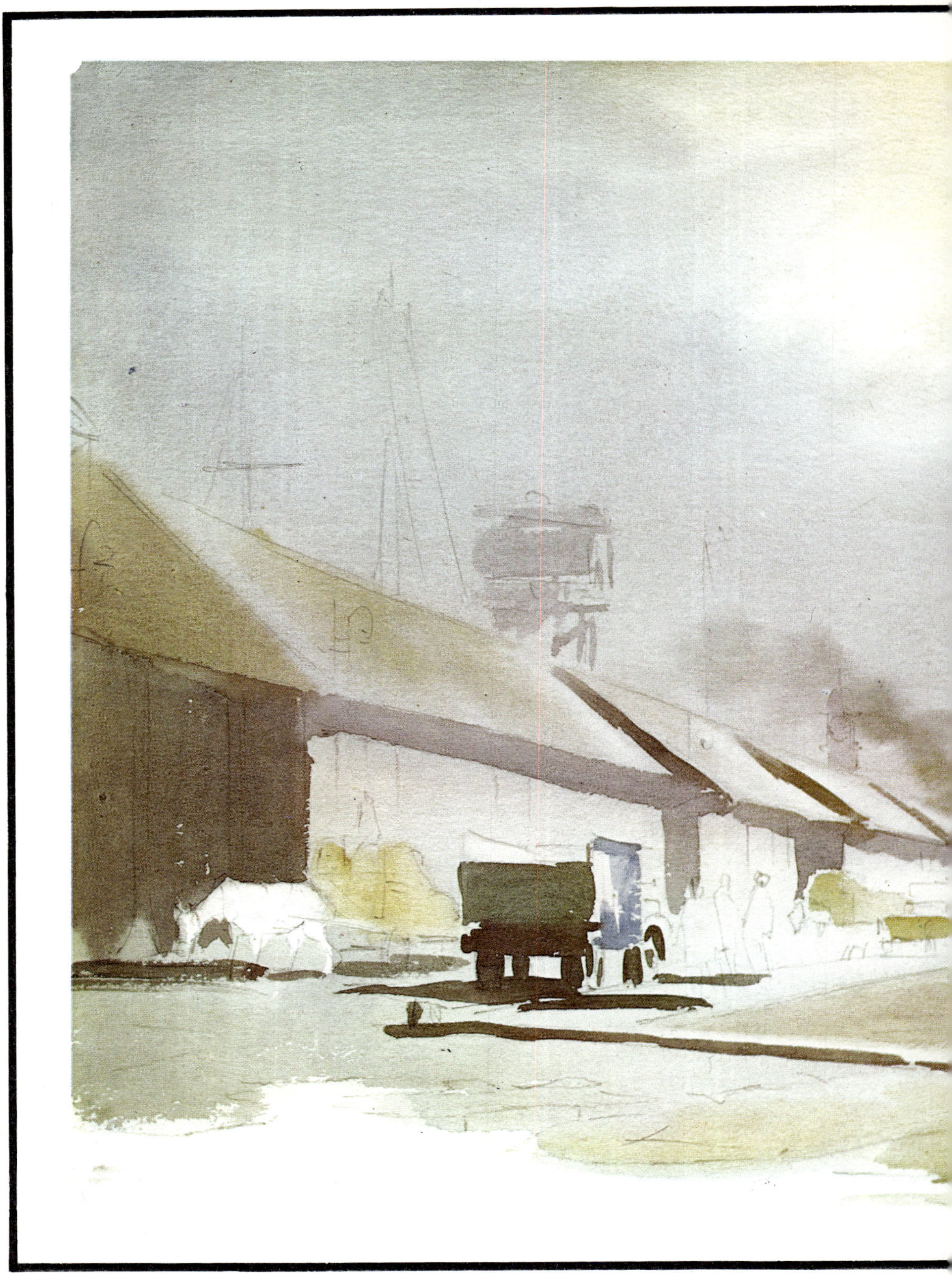

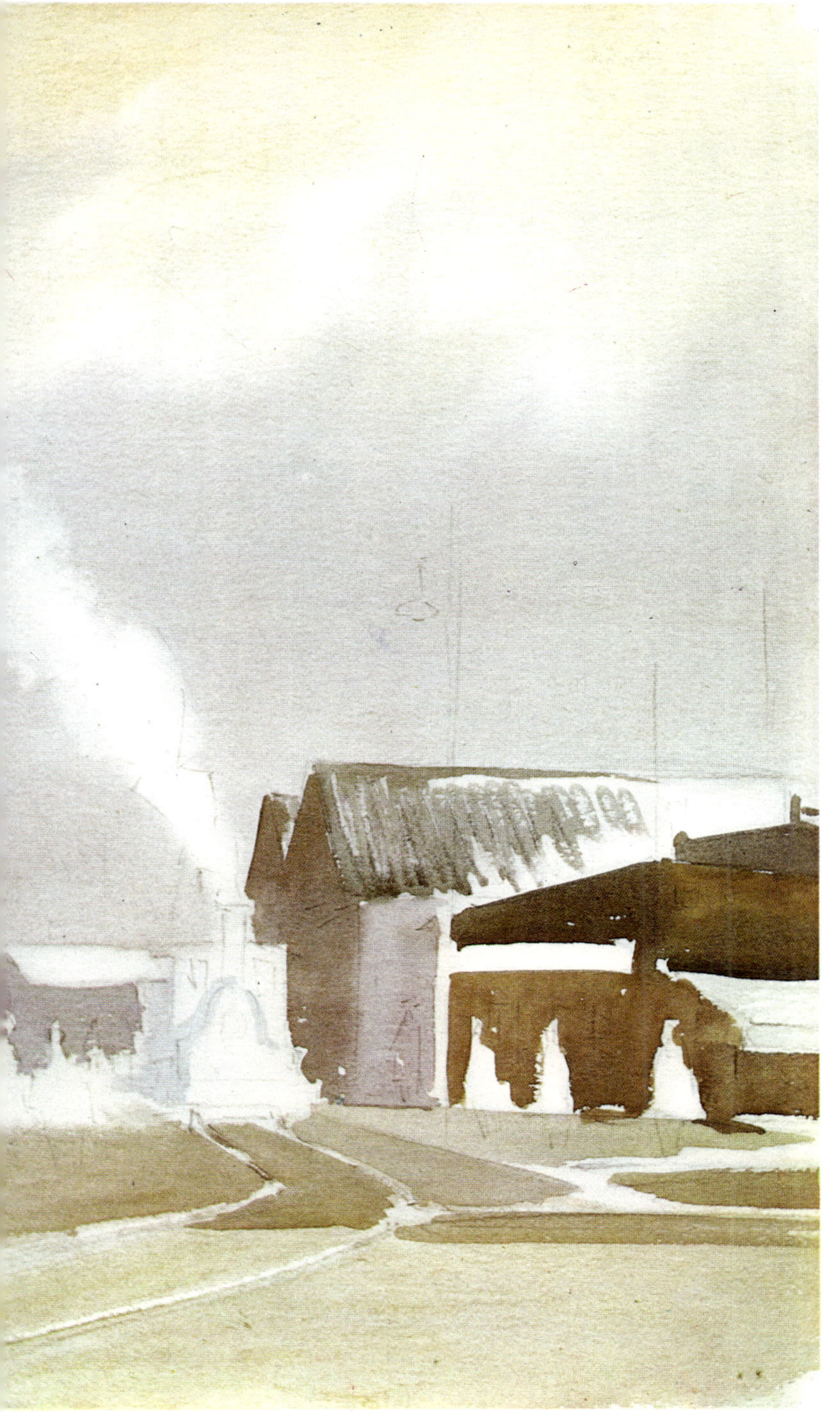

Here is the first stage of the watercolour «Barcelona Port». Follow the instructions in the text which explain how this first stage is reached, studying the colours and the method.

On the one hand, we can see that the sky and some of the shapes in the background have undoubtedly been painted with the «wet» method but, on the other, many areas and shapes (the sheds and their roofs, the vehicles and figures and also the network of cranes) have been done by means of the «dry» technique, producing firm outlines despite the subtle contrast caused by similarity in tones and colours.

11. «Always begin with the sky», Fresquet told us. And this is no exception: all the more so when we realised that the sky plays an important rôle in this picture and must be done straight off and successfully: «If it is O.K. leave it: if not, it must be done again». So, let's start:

First the sky.

THESE ARE THE COLOURS:

12. First of all, we shall study an important general aspect of the colouring: the dominant tone or colour.

The dominant colour is sienna-blue

If you now mix ultramarine (or cobalt blue), burnt sienna and some water, you will at first get a colour which is very similar to many of the painted areas of this picture: a colour ranging from a neutral grey to a warm or cold grey, a dirty blue or a greyish sienna, depending upon which colour is most used in the mixing. Finally, by mixing both colours with a little water, you will get a dark sienna identical or similar to that used by Fresquet for painting figures and dark shadows or forms. Test this yourself.

Dominant colour blue/burnt sienna

13. Speaking of testing, we shall very shortly be explaining how this or that colour is mixed and shall be referring to a «touch», «with a little», «with enough water», etc. without specifying exactly how much water or colour. So we feel the best system would be for you to begin by testing some sample colours, using the scrap of paper earmarked for this purpose.

Testing colours beforehand on a separate piece of paper

CAREFUL! JUST BEFORE YOU START TO PAINT, WET THE PAPER WITH A BRUSH AND CLEAN WATER.

You must do this. Moisten the paper with clean water down to the limit marked with the thick line in Fig. 4. This will enable us easily to blend the outlines which adjoin the sky, as we shall see.

Moisten the area marked in Fig. 4.

THESE ARE THE COLOURS, THIS IS THE ORDER TO BE FOLLOWED:

When following the instructions given below, look at Fig. 5 where the sections or zones mentioned in the text are indicated by A, B, C, etc.

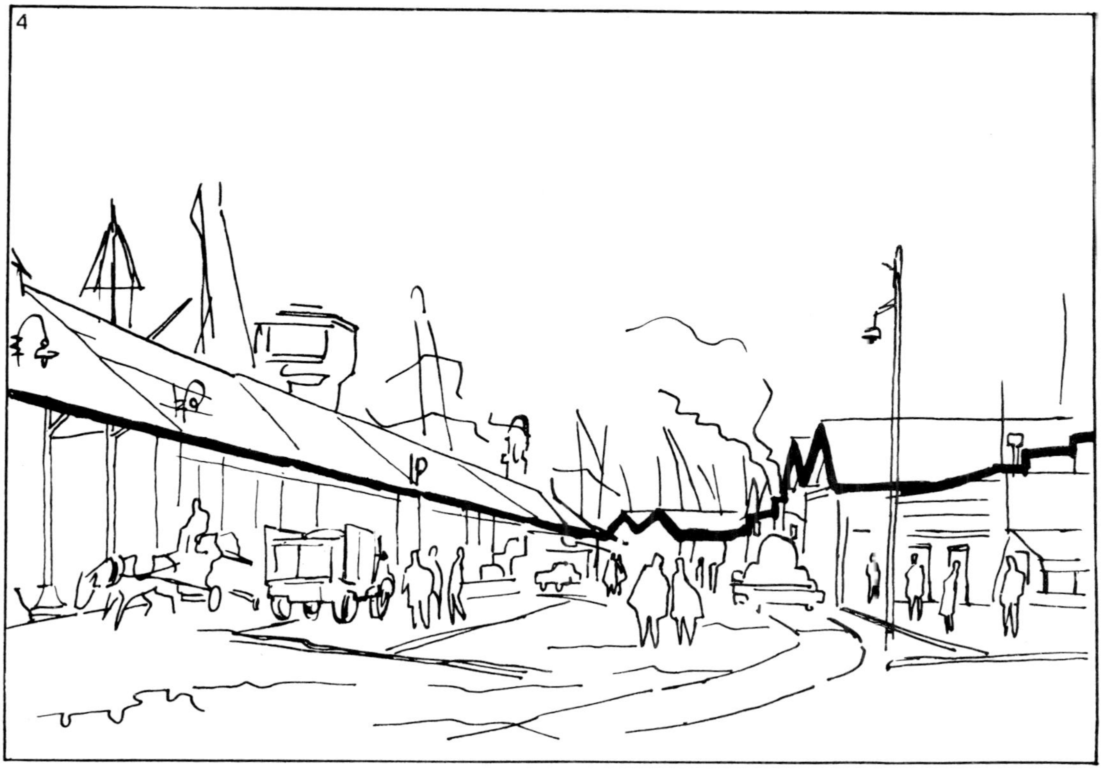

***Sky, right-central area (A): ochre, cobalt blue and red.**

Shading in area A (Fig. 5)

Working on wet paper —this is extremely important— in the centre of the area marked A, apply a «load» of mainly ochre colour, mixed with a little cobalt blue and a very small amount of red. (Careful with the red! It is very strong and can easily dominate the mixture. Remember, ochre is the dominant colour). When this mixture is applied, the water will dilute it, spreading the colour up to more or less the edge area A. (See line). You must help in producing shading so that this predominantly ochre colour is gradually diluted outwards from the line.

***Sky, left and centre (B): cobalt blue and sienna as the basic colours.**

Mix enough of this colour, remembering that it is the basic or dominant colour of the whole sky. Spread this blue-sienna from B, blending it with the ochre when it reaches Area A.

(IMPORTANT: THE SURFACE MUST STILL BE SLIGHTLY WET).

Enriching the basic colour of the sky.

As you mix more of this blue and sienna colour, add very slight —almost imperceptible— touches of carmine, red and green. I mean, within the context of an ABSOLUTE dominant blue-sienna, mix in very slight shades of rose, rose-tinted carmine, very light green... so that the background of the sky is not completely flat: it contains very slight variations —VERY SLIGHT, I repeat— which enrich the general colouring.

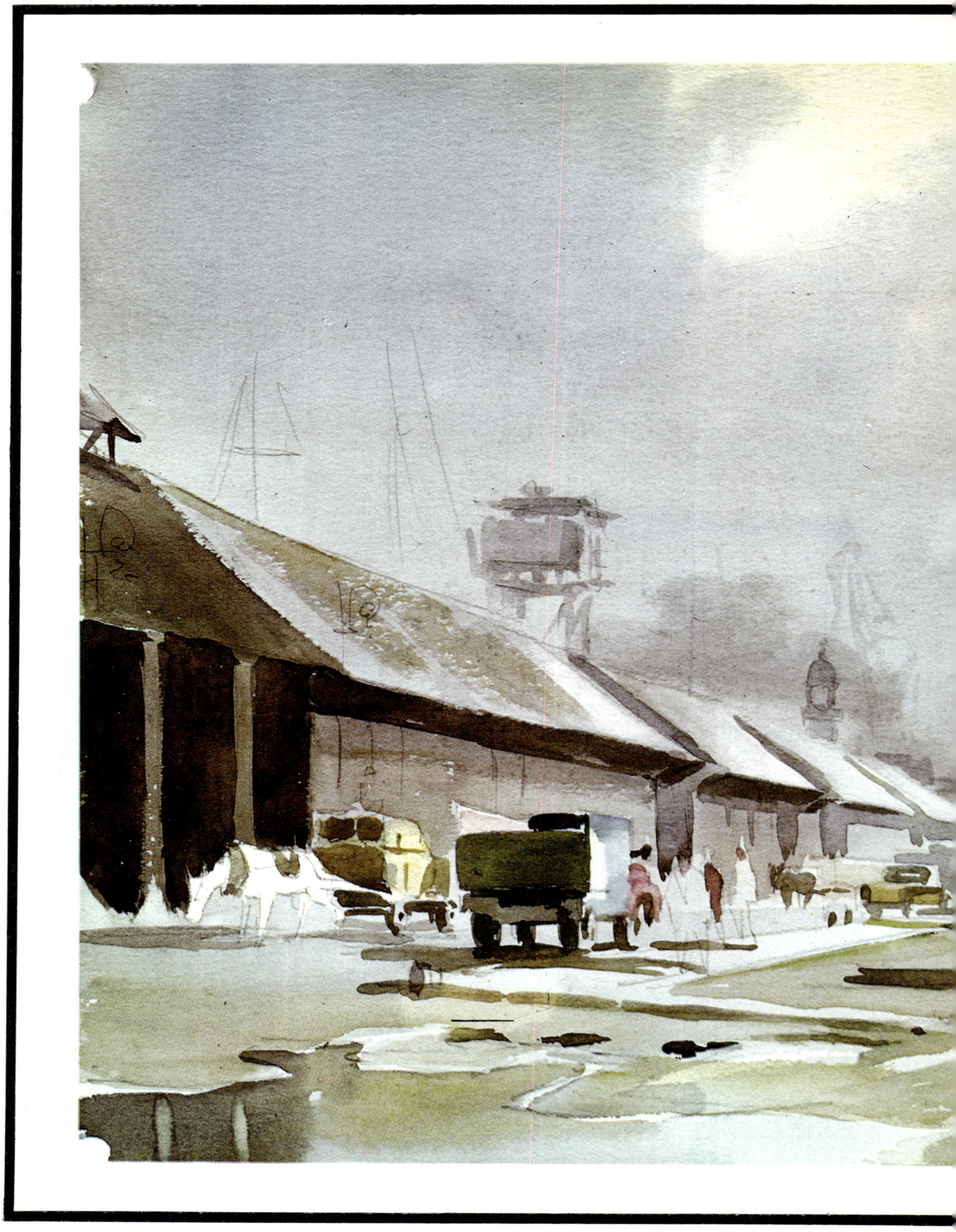

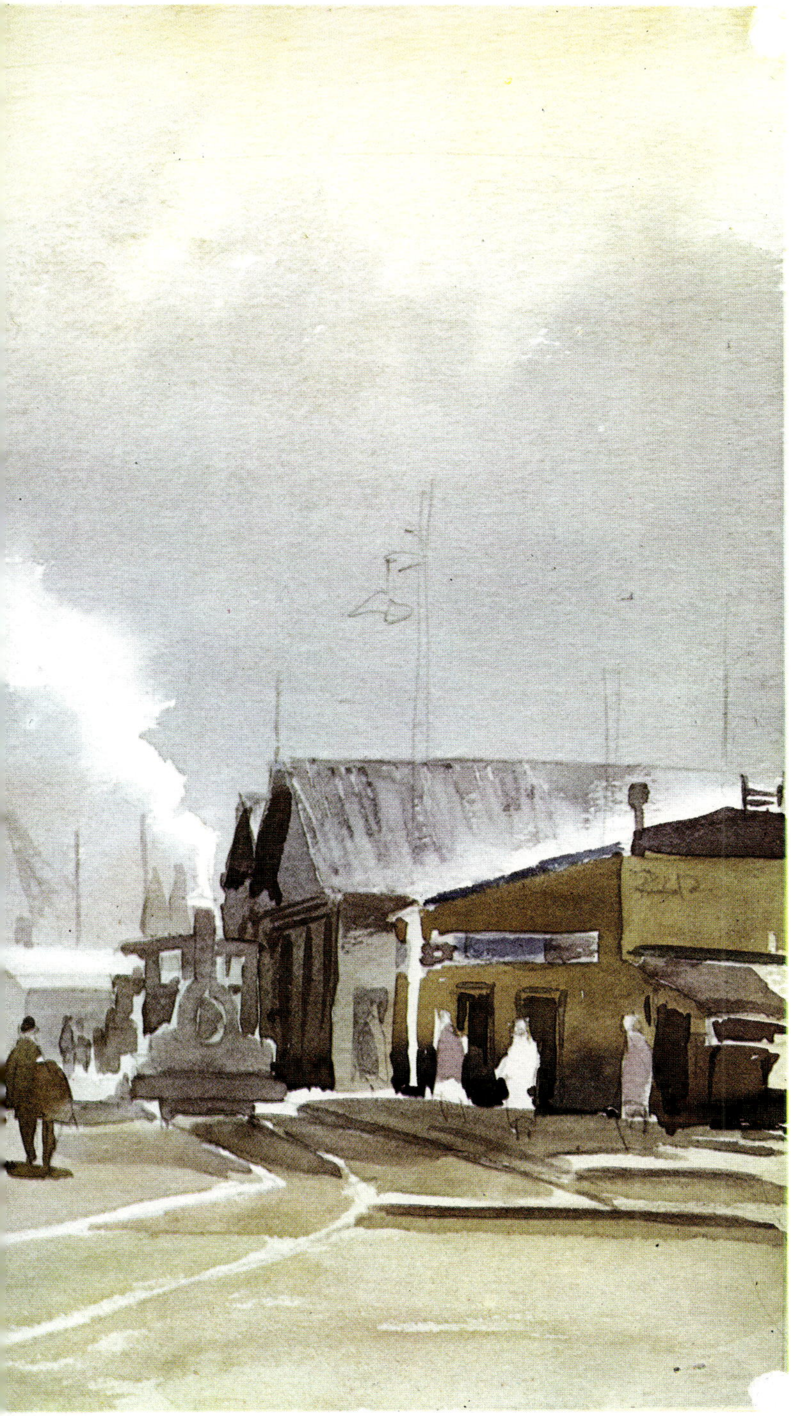

Here you see the colours and tones which your watercolour should have at the second stage. Notice the differences between this and the first stage and also compare it with the large painting, showing the final result.

Engine smoke (C): marked out with a firm outline at the bottom and blended with the sky at the top.

When you reach the smoke from the train, first mark out a white area as shown by C. Try to form a «break» where the edge of this white area approaches the funnel. Then with the brush and clean water, blend the blue-sienna at D with the white of the smoke until the smoke is shaded into the sky.

Mark out the white of the train's smoke.

Smoke on the horizon (E): Ultramarine blue and sienna.

Still working on a wet surface, using a brush loaded with a mixture of ultramarine blue and sienna and a little water, paint in this smoke allowing the wet surface of the sky to merge with this darker tone.

Dark smoke «wet» painted.

Lower edge of the sky (Fig. 6):

As you can see, there are two lines along the lower edge of the sky. Remember here that:

> **The line A (thick line) is the edge of the area first moistened with clean water. The line B (dotted line) is the edge of the blue-sienna of the sky.**

So the blue-sienna has to be brought down to the line B and the colour is then to be shaded and blended in such a way that, at A, the colour has faded out, avoiding an abrupt break.

Shading in the lower edge of the sky.

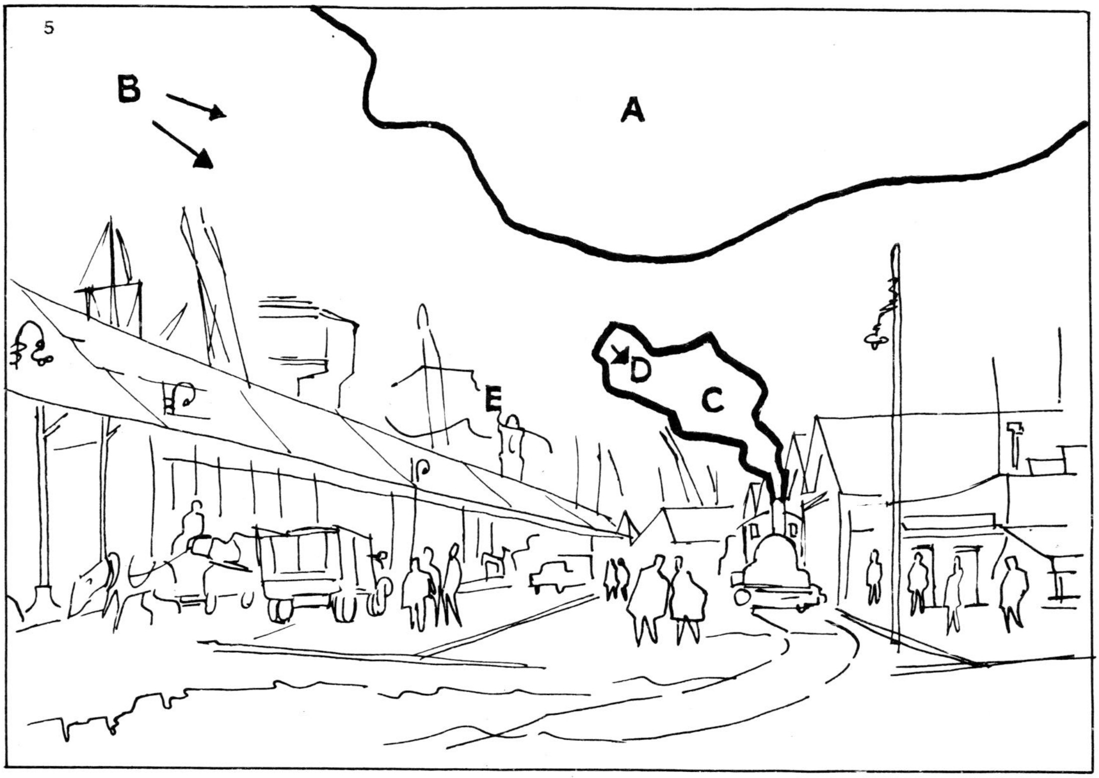

With regard to this area along the horizon, notice that, particularly in the centre, it contains a more obvious mixture of rose-ochre in the blue-sienna which at this point is also slightly lighter.

Sky, right-hand side (F): continue with cobalt blue and sienna as dominant colours.

Complete the sky with this right-hand area using the above colours and repeating the process described earlier.

The sky contains no marked out white area except the smoke from the engine.

Lamp posts and cranes will be painted over the sky.

It can be assumed that both the complex of cranes and the electric lamp post on the right are to be painted on the blue-sienna of the sky without any separate area being marked out in advance.

*

That's the sky finished. How has it gone? As you know, it has to be left like that or be done all over again. However, in case it has to be re-done, Fresquet gives us some remarkable advice, or rather a trick of the trade.

HOW TO REPAINT THE SKY WITHOUT STARTING ON A NEW SHEET OF PAPER.

Imagine that the sky has not come out right the first time, and that it contains «breaks», beads, unevenness, etc. And suppose you have only

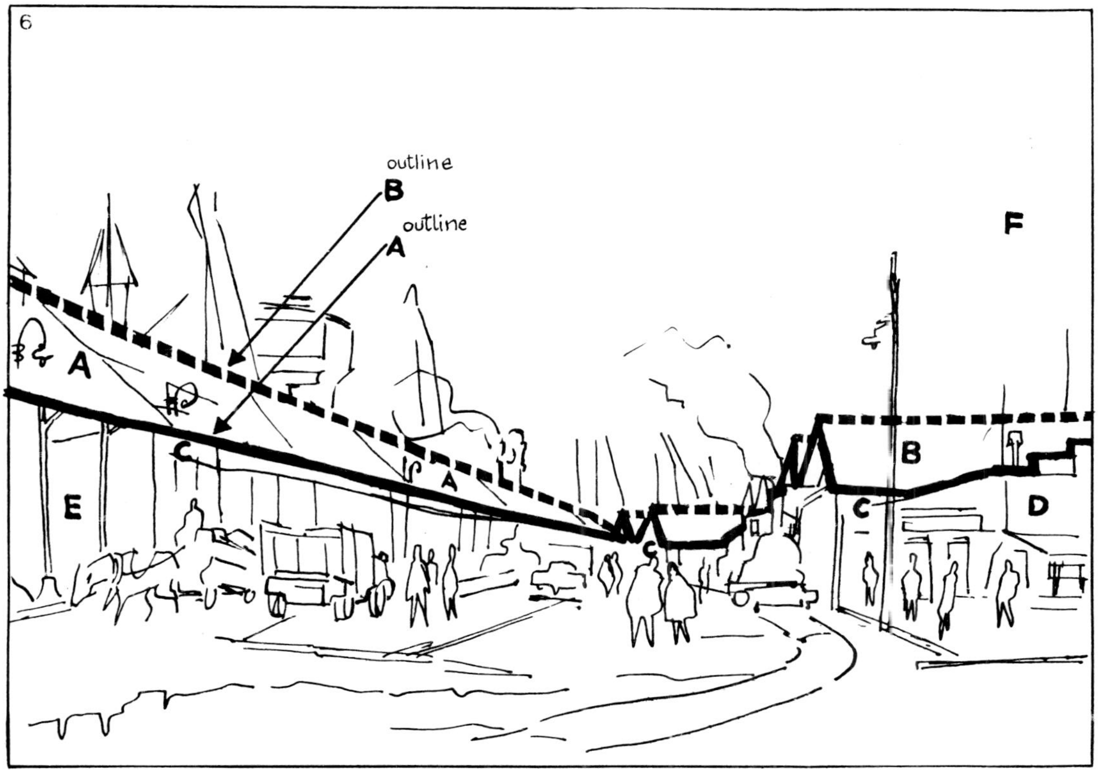

this one sheet of paper or that you don't want to begin all over again, with all the trouble of re-drawing the basic sketch.

There is one way of avoiding this; place the paper in clean water in a tub or sink if you are working at home: or in a pond or river if you are working in the country, letting the water cover the area on which you painted the sky. Dry and wipe it... and repeat this a few times until the water has diluted the washes of the sky and it is clear enough to start afresh. «However», says Fresquet, «remember that this method is not always effective. It is no good if the sky contains a lot of colour or if, in order to dilute the colour, you have made the paper too wet, causing wrinkles which make it difficult to repaint the surface.

Method for «saving» a badly painted sky.

Roofs on the left (Fig. 6, A): Ochre, sienna, ultramarine blue.

Begin by wetting this area with clean water. Then apply ochre-sienna with a touch of ultramarine blue, very little, just enough to make the original ochre-sienna mixture grey.

Roofs on the right (B): Ultramarine blue, sienna, green and black.

The basic colours are ultramarine blue and sienna with the former dominant. But you may need a very small amount of black and an even smaller amount of green. Try it.

Shadows cast by the roofs (C): ultramarine blue, sienna and a little carmine.

You must obtain a greyish purple with a tinge of sienna.

Ground, general: ultramarine blue, ochre, sienna, green, red, carmine.

First a general very pale coat mixed from ultramarine blue, ochre and burnt sienna, producing a rather dirty cream. Then, on the left, add a touch of green, sienna and ultramarine blue. Continue with this colour up to the right-hand foreground, introducing some ochre and a very small amount of red (an extremely small amount, just enough to give it a slight rose tinge). Finish with the most distant areas, using a little more sienna and a little green: if necessary, make it greyer by adding ultramarine blue.

Painting the ground; copy the model

Careful! When painting the ground, you must leave out the white areas shown in the model.

Walls on left (D): sienna, ultramarine blue, green.

The walls of the bar: sienna, green and ultramarine blue to darken them.

Open shed on left (E): sienna, ultramarine blue, green.

Make sure you leave out the shape of the horse.

Lorry, bales, vehicles in background.

The lorry has a dominant green, made grey by adding sienna. The bales on the wagon pulled by the horse: ochre with a touch of blue, just enough to mute the strident yellow of the ochre.

SECOND STAGE (pp. 112-113).

Notice how this stage is produced.

You can almost say that the colours you have mixed in the first stage are sufficient. Or course, because these earlier mixtures will already have shown you which colours play the fundamental part in the artistic unity of this watercolour, namely cobalt or ultramarine blue, depending upon the degree of luminosity or opacity you require. Bear in mind here that while cobalt blue is a neutral blue, ultramarine always has a violet tinge. Both of these blues are almost always mixed with burnt sienna which is the basic colour for obtaining that bluish grey of the sky, and with a burnt sienna dominant in the figures and objects in the remainder of the picture. Ochre and green also occur in some of these objects, the first to introduce a yellow tinge and the second for enriching the mixture. Finally, minimal amounts of red and carmine are used to give a slightly warm feeling in some of the shades. As a last resort, black can be introduced to provide some clean greys.

General summary of the colours used.

Here are a few more examples to support this general summary:

Winches and cranes: ultramarine blue, sienna and carmine.

Ultramarine blue and sienna alone are almost enough but it would be best to add a very light wash of rose-carmine to produce a slight violet tinge. But very little.

Figures in the foreground: sienna, blue and green.

Side and engine of the lorry: ultramarine blue and carmine.

But when painting this blue side and the reddish carmine of the engine, remember that neat colour must not be applied: a very small amount of sienna has to be added to the blue to mute it and a touch of grey (black or light blue) in the carmine for the same purpose.

THIRD AND LAST STAGE (MODEL)

We are not going to talk about the colours any more. We feel sure that you need no more advice in this respect.

So we shall mention a few points concerning the skill called for in this last stage.

Pool in the foreground:

How to paint water and reflections.

Remember the method recommended by Fresquet: first a wash or coat of light colour reflecting the colour of the sky. Then, while it is still wet, add the dark colours reflecting objects and shadows. In this case use sienna, green and ultramarine blue, bringing out the lights, forms and reflections by soaking up colour with your brush.

Ground, general:

As you can see by comparing the illustrations of the previous stages, in this final model, the finished work, the ground has been painted in two, or at the most three successive coats. Notice that the dark areas, corresponding to the shadows, have been «dry»-painted.

Ground: dark areas are «dry» painted.

Lamp post on right.

The lower part of this post was marked out at the beginning. But, as Fresquet found here and there, this marked out area may become covered: if so, you need simply paint the shape of the post with the dark grey and then lighten the lower half with a dry brush, soaking up the tone and colour.

Marking out and soaking up the lamp post.

Final touches with weakened Indian ink, drawing with a wooden spill.

(You know what a wooden spill is: a chip of an ordinary brush-handle cut to a nib at one end and pointed).

Final touches with spill and diluted Indian ink.

If you carefully study Fresquet's watercolour, you can see here and there, as finishing touches, some thick, solid dark lines, almost black: for instance, the curve of the tracks of the approaching train, the outlines of the roofs on the left, the leg and hooves of the horse, etc.

These lines are part of the technique for finishing off this type of classic, clear-cut watercolour, strengthening the outlines and profiles of certain shapes. They are usually drawn in Indian ink, using a wooden spill and the ink is diluted with water so that the lines are not too strong. You should keep a jar of Indian ink wash already made up for adding these effects.

The spill is an ideal means of producing a full dark line or a broken, wide line made by drawing with an almost dry spill, as shown in the wires running from the right-hand post in Fresquet's drawing.

Signing... and fixing.

Signing, of course... but what does «fixing» mean? You can buy a type of watercolour fixer which is used more to brighten the colours than to fix them. We must remember that even really first-class watercolours lose a little of their intensity when dry (this is remarkably obvious with low-quality colours). To restore their initial strength and intensity, we use this fixing varnish.

Fixing varnishes for watercolours.

AND THAT WAS PAINTING IN WATERCOLOURS

To be successful, you must have both the artist's temperament and the labourer's dexterity. You cannot paint well without discipline and obeying the rules. With oils, you can leave the picture and return to it later and bad, impatient work can be put right at a later session when you are calm and collected. But this is impossible with watercolours: impatience is forbidden. You must accept its rules and exacting laws.

The English watercolourist Bacon, has said: «You only master watercolours by obeying their laws».

Watercolours require discipline.

Yet, like Latin in university entrance exams, mastery of this art reveals unsuspected avenues for learning more about drawing and painting.

And also about oil-painting...